T0072299

FROM DETECT TO INTELLECT:
UNCOVERING THE MEMORY SKILLS OF
SHERLOCK HOLMES

CLUES ON HOW TO BE
A MEMORY SLEUTH

DANIEL GUILFOYLE, LCSW-R

BALBOA.PRESS

A DIVISION OF HAY HOUSE

Balboa Press books may be ordered through booksellers or by contacting:

Balboa Press
A Division of Hay House
1663 Liberty Drive
Bloomington, IN 47403
www.balboapress.com
844-682-1282

Print information available on the last page.

ISBN: 979-8-7652-3677-2 (sc)
ISBN: 979-8-7652-3676-5 (e)

Balboa Press rev. date: 12/05/2022

CONTENTS

DEDICATION

To my adoring wife Erin, who continues to love and inspire me each and every day of our marriage. To my brother Matthew, who is the real "Mycroft" to my "Sherlock". To my mother Lynn, who always encouraged my unending thirst for knowledge. To Dominic O'Brien, the man that inspired me towards my timeless "journey" into the field of memory improvement. To my late stepfather Steve, I love you and miss you dearly each day. And finally to Sir Arthur Conan Doyle, who without such a literary genius, this world would have been deprived of being a part of the timeless and classic adventures of the greatest consulting detective in the world, Mr. Sherlock Holmes.

INTRODUCTION

Hello everyone, nice to meet you. Please allow me to introduce myself, as I am sure that most of you are unfamiliar with me. My name is Daniel Guilfoyle, and I am the author of a previous book on memory improvement, entitled "**From Shrink to Think: A Mental Journey through the Memory Journey**". In this book, I introduced myself as a "shrink" who had decided to embark upon a "journey" into the world of memory improvement. I went over various techniques and methods of cognitive enhancement, as well as regaling you with some stories of my childhood, and how each story related to my unforeseeable destiny to achieve memory mastery. For those of you, who were not able to purchase this piece of literature, please let me start by re-introducing myself and explaining to you why I chose to write this second book on memory improvement.

As I previously stated, my name is Daniel Guilfoyle, and I am a "shrink", or more specifically, a licensed clinical social worker (LCSW-R). Rather than overwhelm you with the terminology and vocabulary needed to understand such a profession, let me try to summarize what it is that I do for a living. I have a Bachelor's Degree in Sociology, and a Master's Degree in Social Work. I have spent numerous years providing mental health therapy to a barrage of different clients in various settings, such as clinics, schools, and even a men's prison. Throughout my 17 year professional career, I have learned many clinical skills, such as cognitive therapy, behavior therapy, group therapy, crisis interventions, solution focused therapy, and play therapy. After having passed three national licensure examinations over the course of my career, I am now able to call myself a fully qualified psychotherapist, or in this case, a "shrink".

For most of my adult career, I would simply do what most other rational adults would do when they had to go to work. I would get up out of bed, get showered, get dressed, grab my lunch, give my wife a kiss goodbye, and then leave for work in the morning. During the course of the day, I would engage in many social work related tasks, such as writing notes, speaking to clients, conferring with colleagues, and managing my phones and emails. Some days were easy; other days were down right stressful. Sometimes I would get the chance to enjoy my lunch, other days I would come home sick. All in all, never in my whole life did I ever imagine that one day, without warning, I would embark upon the greatest "cognitive" *discovery* of my life.

It was not until I was almost 37 years old, did I finally have my first real brush with memory improvement. It was a dark chapter in my life, as I was working at a maximum security men's prison. Each and every day, I was exposed to countless instances of dangerous situations. Things like violently aggressive inmates, sadistic prison guards, unhealthy room conditions, countless security checks, and impending layoffs, consistently plagued my mind at each and every turn. Just when I thought that things could not get any worse, something else would later happen that would push me further and further down that dark hole in my psyche. I was afraid that I would never be able to crawl back out of this pit of hell that I was trapped in. Needless to say, I knew that I needed to get some help.

It was then that I went to see a therapist of my own. This person helped guide me back to some semblance of normalcy, by teaching me specific coping skills such as stress management, deep breathing, and my all-time favorite technique of all; guided imagery. In this technique, my therapist asked me to visualize a "happy place" of my own, where I was free to walk around anywhere I wanted to. Then she asked me to take notice of the things that I saw during my journey. I picked an old home that I used to live in as a child, and was able to see myself moving around freely from room to room, as if I was just floating around in the air. I took notice of the various items that I remembered being placed in each room. After this exercise was over, I started to notice that not only was I feeling much calmer and relaxed, but that my brain and mind both seemed to be much more focused and alert at the moment.

It was then that I started to become interested in the topic of memory improvement. So I decided to do some research and eventually looked up how such a simple meditation-like technique, could possibly have helped me to be able to reach such an improved state of mind. I looked up books on memory improvement, from variously accomplished national and world champion competitors. One of these competitors is a man who I feel I will be indebted to for the rest of my life. He is a man whose memory technique for memorizing numbers will be discussed later in the book.

During the next couple of years of my life, I started to compete at national and online tournaments, where I was pitted against some of the greatest memory champions I have ever met. I was instructed on how to do various related memory tricks, such as memorizing cards, words, names and faces, numbers, letters, personal information, and book related information. I realized that during this time, the more I practiced these techniques, the greater I seemed to get at them. My mind was doing things that I thought were virtually impossible. At one point, I almost felt as though I was of a genius "intellect". But my journey was far from over.

Just when I thought that I could not be inspired anymore by anyone else in this world, another "genius intellect" came into my life in the most unexpected way. I was sitting down to watch TV one day, when I happened to be going through the channels, and came across a TV station called "BBC". I had never really watched that channel before, but I knew that it was famous for showing different British television programs that I had enjoyed watching when I was younger. Yet on this one particular day, I just happened to catch an episode of a remake of a very popular British television series, which has been on TV before in many different forms. And that specific television program was entitled "Sherlock Holmes". This was the newer version of the Sherlock Holmes series that aired on BBC from 2010-2018. And the character that intrigued me most, was the main character known as Sherlock Holmes.

This was not the first time in my life that I had been introduced to the infamously gifted consulting detective from the city of London. As a child, I had watched various TV programs with other actors who portrayed the legendary investigator on camera. And I was very much intrigued by the many different facets of the life of the most famous literary sleuth the world has ever known. From things such as his well-known magnifying glass, his love of different types of tobacco, to his incredible deductive and reasoning abilities, each and every episode of these timeless classics seemed like an adventure in of itself. However as a child, I failed to fully grasp the importance of the talents and qualities that made Sherlock Holmes such an invincible opponent to anyone who was willing to try to get away with a major crime in late 19th century England.

It wasn't until I got older did I finally start to realize some of the other incredible traits that made up the psyche of Sherlock Holmes. Some of his most admirable qualities were his amazing analytical abilities, his inhuman ability to pay attention to specific details at various crime scenes, his encyclopedic knowledge of different subjects of study, and his remarkable determination to see each and every case through to its inevitable conclusion. But the one thing that truly fascinated me the most about the character of Sherlock Holmes was his somewhat *superhuman memorizing abilities*.

It seemed as though there were times when Holmes himself could not forget a single detail about a case that he worked on. Whether it be the personal information of an individual that he spoke to earlier, or just the facts that he read from a newspaper article only months ago, it simply did not matter. Holmes just seemed to have an inhuman ability to recall specific data whenever he liked. No matter what evidence was presented to him, whether it was furniture items around the room, or the smell of tobacco on another man's shirt, Holmes had an interesting capacity to be able to hold onto and store such information in his head without much effort, and then recall such information later at the moment when it was most needed. You have to wonder how such a person was capable of such incredible feats of memory.

In this book, I would like to explore with you some of the various methods of memory improvement that I have learned through my years as a memory competitor and author. Then I would like to illustrate to you how Sherlock Holmes was able to use these very same methods in his own personal "journeys" towards solving the most baffling crimes in all of Scotland Yard. Throughout this book, I will teach you how to use your brain in ways similar to the great consulting detective, by explaining time honored memory techniques that are sure to help you become a greater *"mental sleuth"*. You will also be given various exercises and homework assignments that you yourself can use to hone your abilities and skills in the real world. And in addition, I will also give you some tidbits of information that you can use in order to better improve your ability to look, listen and pay attention to your natural surroundings.

And so, with that in mind, please relax and take a deep breath. Come inside the infamous office space of 221B Baker Street NW and get ready for a new adventure into the field of memory. Let's gets ready to take a deeper look inside the complex and "intelligent" mind of the most famous literary "genius" of all time, **_Mr. Sherlock Holmes_**. (And the game is afoot).

CHAPTER 1

THE GENIUS OF SHERLOCK HOLMES

Before we start to explore the various wonders of the mind of the infamous consulting detective, let me first staff off by explaining that **I am not a licensed memory coach or a certified cognitive training specialist.** I am also **not a national ranked memory champion**, though I have competed in several memory competitions before. And finally, **I am not an expert on Holmeisan theory or deduction,** as this type of expertise takes years to master.

In addition, **<u>I DO NOT CLAIM TO HAVE ANY RIGHTS, OWNERSHIP, OR PROPRIETORSHIP</u>, of any Sherlock Holmes' related materials or studies** as most of the information that you will be presented with comes from his various books and stories. However, despite my lack of qualifications, I too was once completely unaware of the field of memory improvement. I was someone who was just starting out new in this particular area of study, and had no idea what to expect. And I had no idea about how the field of memory could possibly be applied to the study of the methodology of the great Sherlock Holmes.

And so, throughout the course of these upcoming chapters, I will be offering you my own personal "consulting services" in regards to the exploration of the field of memory mastery. As you read through this book, you will find several interesting patterns that I have specifically included so as to provide you with a more comprehensive sense of the subject. First, instead of giving you lots of technical terminology and related tales, I will speak to you both <u>directly and in conversational mode</u>. In this way, I want to make you feel comfortable enough so that you are able to understand and comprehend what I am saying as if I were almost sitting right across from you.

Second, I have included many bits of side humor throughout the chapters, to help lessen the anxiety accompanied through certain exercises and lessons. Both Holmes and I can agree on at least one thing when it comes to doing actual work with the brain; it is important to find a little humor in any given situation. But as Sherlock Holmes would say "I cannot live without brainwork".

Third, I have also included many different phrases, terms, ideas and important concepts throughout most of the text. Such information will either be <u>underlined</u> or listed in **bold print**. While this might seem somewhat distracting in nature, don't get too caught up in the actual differences between print and font.

Finally, I have included specific tests and homework assignments for you to work on at your own convenience after each lesson on memory improvement. Holmes himself would agree that it is important to work on some type of related self-reflective homework at any given time. No matter what academic subject or infamous criminal case he might be working on, Sherlock was always keen on learning about his own personal strengths and weaknesses.

And finally, towards the end of this book, I will be providing you with some words of wisdom, motivation and encouragement, as well as certain things that you yourself can do in your personal life to try to be a little more like the genius detective himself. I have always felt that it is vitally important to make sure that the reader feels safe and comfortable enough to disengage from the written materials that they are reading. So that they can finally go off into the real world and use their proverbial "magnifying glass" of memory in whatever endeavors they so choose to do so.

Now then, let's get back to meeting the man that we have all been waiting to hear about; the one, the only, **<u>Mr. Sherlock Holmes</u>**. I first heard about this well-known logistic legend when I was a young man growing up in the town of Goshen. I remember watching a TV program on BBC with a famous actor, who stared in the short lived

1980's TV series "Sherlock Holmes". At first, I was not aware of who the main character was, or what his role was in terms of helping to solve crimes in late 19th century London. I also did not understand how his magnificent brain was able to come up with such incredible conclusions to some of the most baffling and puzzling crimes at the time. Only then was I about to realize the true genius of the man who would one day revolutionize not only the field of forensic science, but also the business of cognitive enhancement itself.

In order to give you a better description of the persona of Sherlock Holmes, lets first start off by going over a few of his own personal traits and qualities. First, Sherlock could be described as a man who truly was dedicated to the craftsmanship of his own work. He was not overly concerned with simply being able to solve major cases, or to astound people with his deductive skills. Instead, he only wanted to continue to pursue each criminal case with such tenacity and vigor, that at times it almost appeared as though he was somewhat obsessed with the finer details of the crime itself.

Next, due to his inherent desire to always challenge his mind, Holmes hated the idea of boredom, procrastination or stagnation. In other words, his mind was always craving mental stimulation wherever he could find it. Whether it be analyzing the type of blood stains on the shoes of a murder victim, to determining what type of financial affairs his colleague had engaged in the night before, Holmes's mind "rebelled" against inactivity, as he usually requested his constituents to find him new "puzzles" to work on.

In addition, while most of us are satisfied to learn only certain amounts of information on just one or two subjects, Sherlock was a modern day "polymath" of random knowledge. To be more clinical, the term "polymath" is used to describe an individual who possesses an expert knowledge on at least three or more different subjects of study at any given time. People like Leonardo Da Vinci, John Van Neumann, and Nicola Tesla, were polymaths in their own right. Each person would continuously try to consume more and more materials about random fields of study that were of interest to them.

Holmes himself was said to have had a great understanding of at five major academic topics, such as criminal literature, chemistry, musical composition, geography, and human anatomy. Other subjects, such as astronomy, economics, and oceanography, were of no concern to Sherlock, as he often would tell people that such information would not be helpful to him in order to solve various murder cases throughout the country. He felt that there was only a limited space in his "attic" of memory to store such information.

Most of us are keenly aware of one of the most impressive abilities of the great Sherlock Holmes, and that was his outstanding level of observational and situational awareness. This was something that he brought with him during each and every case that he worked on, both inside and outside of his apartment. No matter where he was going or what he was doing, Holmes always made it a point to pay attention to all of the details that surrounded him. Whether it be the scent of the perfume worn by a certain female companion, to the lining of the pants worn by a uniformed officer at the scene of a crime, Holmes almost always was consciously aware of his surroundings at all given times. He also realized how such surroundings were relevant towards discovering the cause or origin of any related crime around him.

But one thing that many of us were not always so aware of was the fact that Sherlock Holmes had an amazing ability to memorize information that was presented to him. In most of his stories, Sherlock is able to remember random bits of information regarding various cases that he has either worked on or has read about in the newspaper. By being able to recall these vast amounts of miscellaneous facts at any given time, Sherlock was almost always able to determine if the information that was being presented to him, was somehow relevant to information that he had already stored in his brain for future references.

Whether it be remembering what type of food a certain suspect used to eat years ago, or the subject of a conversation he had with a colleague several weeks earlier, Sherlock never failed when it came to being able to remember certain pieces of previously learned information, and then determining how such knowledge was connected or "linked" to another piece of more current information that was being presented to him. In other words, it seemed as though he was able to link information that he already knew, to information that he was about to know.

In most of his stories, Holmes is well known for remembering many different facts about cases that he has read about in the newspapers, and then to be able to recall such details with flawless ease. There were many times in the course of his adventures, when he would be standing at the scene of a crime, and would take notice of a random detail that the rest of the police were not consciously aware of. And from looking at that one particular detail, Holmes would be able to "link" such information presented to him, to another case that he had already read about years ago. Other times, Holmes would make a conscious effort to remember the details of a former case that he had worked on, so that he could be more prepared if he should happen to stumble upon a similar case in the future.

In this book, we are going to focus on several different topics of memory, all of which are based upon some of the variously diverse fields that Holmes himself was known for studying. Subjects such as medicine, clothing, literature, historical dates, addresses, directions, names and faces, personal information, numbers, and vocabulary words, are just some of the different areas of interest that Holmes liked to memorize when he was preparing to take on another major case set before him.

And based upon some of the lessons from my previous book, as well as a few new lessons in this current book, you are going to be able to learn how to better memorize all of these random subjects of memory, using time honored techniques that memory experts have been using for centuries. So, without further ado, light up your favorite pipe, put on your trademark deerstalker hat, pull out your trusted magnifying glass, and get ready to deep a "journey" into the celebrated and gifted mind of the legendary detective, Mr. Sherlock Holmes.

CHAPTER 2

THE BRAIN ATTIC AND OTHER RELATED MEMORY TECHNIQUES

When I was younger, we lived in a house in a quiet part of Middletown, NY. I remember that there were times when my parents were busy downstairs with their own respective chores. During such time my brother and I used to sneak up to the attic located next to one of our bedrooms. We would climb up the staircase and switch on the overhead light. Once we finally got up to the top of the stairs, we were greeted with the site of a rather large pile of old boxes that my father had stored up in the crawl space. Each box was clearly labeled with various words and numbers, denoting the subject of the contents of each box. All boxes were neatly staffed, one on top of another, in either alphabetical order or numerical order. And even though these containers were covered with layers of cobwebs and dust, it appeared that whatever materials were located inside of them were obviously meant to be organized in a specific order that I could not begin to understand.

Most of us, who grew up in a house with more than a few bedrooms and some adequate closet space, are very familiar with such a scenario as the one that was previously mentioned. No matter where you lived or what you owned, there was just never enough room to keep all of your materials in one place at one time. That is the bedrock of the concept known as a "storage space". A storage space is generally any area of your home or residence, where you have enough room to pack up and enclose any major belongings or personal artifacts that you want into variously different containers. You are not likely to spend each and every day sorting through such materials or cleaning out the available space. It is always good to know that there is usually just one specific location in your home or "palace" where you can keep all of your most important and personal items from your life. That way, whenever you need to find those items, you always know where to look.

I especially enjoy utilizing such a concept at my own house as well as my office. At my home, I have many boxes that I have stored both in the basement and the attic for different reasons. Some boxes are big, some boxes are small. Some are located on top of shelves; others are located in cabinets or dressers. Some boxes are taped up; others are tied down with strings. Overall, there is one universal thing that I chose to do with all of these boxes that are kept throughout my house; and that is that I will always *organize them* into a specific pattern that only makes sense to me based upon my own personal needs.

I also do the same thing at my office where I work as a social worker. Although I do not have enough space for boxes and containers at such location, I do have some space for files and folders that I keep both inside and on top of my desk. On my desk, I have folders that are within eyesight of me, all of which are labeled and color coded, depending upon the subject matter. Other folders and files are located within the drawers of my desk, usually with specific name tags hanging on the edges of them. All of these files and folders are organized alphabetically, numerically, or just in a specific order that is used for my own personal needs. All in all, I have turned my tiny office space, into my own personal "file cabinet" of social work related information.

For most of my life, people used to think that I was obsessive about details, or just overly concerned about order and cleanliness. Whether it was just a part of my personality, or simply just good family training inbreeded into my mind, I cannot truly be certain of why I was the way I was. All that I know is that I craved organization and structure, no matter what activities I was going through. Whether I was preparing for a major class in school, getting ready for a large project at work, or dealing with some personal family crisis at home, the results were always the same; I loved to organize things.

I would always tackle each situation in the same manner; by both preparing for any challenges that came my way through keeping all related information at my disposal in case I needed it. Much like a file cabinet helps most people to better be able to keep records and papers in a specific order, I operated in much the same way in most capacities in my life. I suppose that I tended to model my "attic" storage place in the same manner as the human brain.

Sherlock Holmes was well known for using a particular catchphrase to describe his ability to store and retrieve pieces of information from inside his mind. He often referred to the particular storage center of his brain, as a "brain attic". If you can remember from the previous example that I gave you about the boxes that I had in my own childhood attic, imagine if your brain could function in the same way. Picture if you could somehow to be able to "store" various categories of information inside of your brain in an orderly fashion. You would make sure that such information remains in its desired location until you are ready to "retrieve" it. Whether it be thinking about a certain word, name, number, date, event, or image, just think about what it would be like if your brain could operate in a capacity similar to a storage space or a file cabinet. You would have a plethora of information right at your fingertips, just waiting for you to retrieve it a moment's notice.

Throughout the literary stories of Sherlock Holmes, as well as various episodes of TV shows and movies, the main character is portrayed as a man with an incredible memory and an almost superhuman ability to remember and retrieve pieces of information out of his head. Sometimes he was able to do so at the scene of a crime, other times he was capable of recalling such information while lounging in his favorite chair or smoking a pipe. Whatever the circumstances were, Sherlock was always able to remember some valuable piece of information that would serve a greater purpose while he was in the process of investigating a case in the area. It seems as though Sherlock just loved to make sure that he had the right information in his head for the right reasons.

However, Sherlock was also keenly aware not to remember too much information about all different subjects in his head. He often was very selective and particular about what information he was prepared to input into his "brain attic" so as to not overcrowd it. On one occasion, his associate Dr. John Watson, was prepared to explain to him some information regarding the subject of astronomy. While Holmes found the subject to be somewhat fascinating, he chose to ignore the speech in its entirety. He made great efforts to forget such information for future reference, as he felt that knowing about astronomy would serve no purpose in his quests to solve various crimes throughout London. In a way, he was selective about what information he felt was to be of good use to him for all future endeavors.

Holmes was not the kind of person who simply allowed all bits and pieces of information to enter his brain at a moment's notice. He would in fact specifically filter out certain types of information that he felt would be of no use to him at a later date, and would only hold onto information that he believed would be of value to him at another time. Plus, he also made sure that whatever information he chose to remember and store in his "brain attic", he would also prepare to organize such information into various subjects and categories that he felt were most relevant to his own personal needs. In other words, he would literally create his own mental "filing cabinet" which he would carry with him in his head.

Even though he was not aware of it at the time, the methods and techniques that Holmes was using to store and retrieve information within his endlessly vast "brain attic", are methods that have been used for centuries by mnemonists, autodidacts, renaissance thinkers, geniuses, memory athletes, and other specially gifted members of the academic elite. Whether or not Holmes was consciously aware of the specific terminology used to describe the systems that he was employing when attempting to rehearse and access certain pieces of information, is not known at this time. What is known is that the very same methods that he was using in his everyday quests to solve various murders throughout the country, are the very same methods that you will be instructed on in the next coming chapters.

The point is that, whether you believe it or not, these particular mnemonic devises and skills are things that all of us can easily do anytime we want to. And throughout this book, I will be going over **3 DIFFERENT MNEMONIC TECHNIQUES** that are the center piece of all memory improvement. And they are called: **the Method of Loci, the Link Method, and the Substitution Method**. For now, in this particular chapter of the book, I will be going over the three main methods of memorization.

The <u>first</u> method that I will be going over with you in regards to memory improvement, is probably the single most important and effective strategy needed to achieve memory mastery in the world. And that particular mnemonic device is called **the Memory Palace, or the Method of Loci**. In this particular method, in order for you to be able to memorize the actual order and pattern of various pieces of information, you must first be able to find a way to make sure that such information is stored in a specific location, or in this instance, a storage area used for the purposes of future recall. Remember from the previous section where I talked about a "brain attic"? Well, in this instance, you will instead be creating a memory "palace" to store most of your memories. But don't worry; you don't have to actually build a real "palace" for such demonstrations.

The method of loci is also referred to as the **Memory journey**, **Memory palace**, or **mind palace technique**. This method is a mnemonic device that was used back in ancient Greek and Roman times, during which most major buildings or residences were constructed in the shape of palaces. In regards to this particular technique, the person would first have to memorize the layout of some particular "palace" building, the arrangement of houses on a street, or any geographical location which was comprised of numerous objects located inside of it. And then the person would have to try to mentally recall where each room or domestic article was positioned in relation to another, such as doors, walls, steps and windows. In this way, the person would be mentally walking through the architecture and layout of their own particular palace of memory, without ever having to physically move through it.

But before we get too far into a discussion about the Memory Palace technique, lets first get an idea about the history of such a mnemonic concept. The idea of a "memory palace" goes back all the way to the days of the ancient Greeks and Romans. It was from there that the origins of the Memory palace technique would come to actually change history forever. One of the earliest known stories about the usage of the Memory palace technique comes from the story of **Simonides of Ceos**, a famous and powerful early Greek philosopher. This story describes in detail the birthplace and origins of this unique memory system. However, not all stories about ancient Greek are full of happiness and glory.

According to legend, after being invited to a banquet to recite a poem to a group of guests, the poet Simonides of Ceos chanted out loud the lyrics to such poem. However, he did not finish the rest of such stance, for he claimed that he had already memorized the poem and did not need to continue. But when his host stated that he would only pay him half of what was owed to him if he did not finish the rest of the sermon, Simonides decided not to honor such request. It was during that time that Simonides was also hosting a large party at one of his famous yet dilapidated banquet halls. He had purposely and previously arranged and organized which rooms and seats each person was assigned to sit in.

He then asked that each person remain in their respective areas for the duration of the party. There were dozens and dozens of fellow guests at his party, some of whom he had never met before. A few moments after everyone had arrived, Simonides was given a message that two men were waiting outside the banquet hall in order to speak with him. So Simonides went outside to speak to these men and find out what their business was.

All of a sudden, without any warning, an earthquake occurred and the ground itself shook. At that moment, the banquet hall roof crashed on top of his guests, killing all of them almost instantly. Simonides was powerless to stop the eventual carnage occurring to his party guests. The victims were so badly injured that they were not identifiable to family due to their wounds, and most people were too afraid to go into the rubble to locate any of their missing loved one.

Yet Simonides was able to aide in the identification of all of the members of his party, by means of recalling the exact location of where each person sat during the banquet, and where their bodies were later located. Eventually, he was able to positively identify the names and locations of all of the houseguests in his banquet hall on that terrible day, without making a single mistake. Wow, such a tragic tale seemed to have such a unique impact upon the world.

For those of us who are not familiar with the dynamics of such a mnemonic technique, let me explain how it is done. First, try to imagine yourself walking through a large house or room that you are inherently familiar with. You don't have to physically "walk" through such a location, as most times it is difficult to be able to actually travel to all of the previous homes and residences that were once very memorable to you. It could be something like your neighbor's house, your grandmother's apartment, your sibling's place of work, or your old school classrooms. All you have to do is make sure that the location you are trying to visualize is large, detailed and graphically vivid in your mind.

Once you are mentally inside such location, try to "walk" along the walls or outer area of such room, and take notice of whatever materials or objects seem to keep your eye. Perhaps you first remember spotting the entrance way door to the room. Then you chose to turn either right or left, and then you come across a large piece of furniture. After that you move onto seeing maybe a door or a window, and so on and so forth, until you have covered the entire area of the house or the building, one room after another. In this way, you are "journeying" through a location that will eventually become one of your memory palaces.

You don't have to actually be an architect or an interior designer to remember the exact layout of the entire building or residence. Just try to remember what you think the actual house or home looked like from your own personal memory. Nobody will be able to read your mind or tell you that you were wrong about the interior or exterior features of such location. And some houses or homes can be quite simple and boring when you try to think about them, leaving you with little information to recall about the design of each house. This is not meant to be an exercise in architecture or interior design. This is just simply a way to give you the appropriate "storage places" needed to eventually store your memories for a future date and time.

After you have mentally "walked" through your fictional house or building, one room after another, next try to take notice of the actual order of the things that you remember seeing as you walked from one location to another. Perhaps you saw the entry door to the room first, then the furniture second, then the window third, and so on. Go back and forth through such "memory palace" at least a few times until you start to feel comfortable with the exact "route" that you took from one room to the next. This will help so that you don't get confused and miss one location or "loci". Once you have done this a few times, you should feel comfortable with your own particular "memory palace" and know each and every room by heart. At this point, when it comes to memorizing materials effectively, you are definitely headed in the right "direction".

By being able to mentally transport yourself throughout the various rooms and locations inside of your fictional "palace", you have now created the appropriate "storage facility" to place all of your future materials to be memorized. In order to better understand the miracle of navigating through the memory palace more clearly, just try to imagine yourself driving a car on the same route each and every day for a long time. After a while, you start to go through what is commonly referred to as "**auto pilot**". This means that you don't remember even getting into the car in the first place. You only remember that you somehow ended up at your final destination without any real memory of how you got there.

Now try to imagine that one of the streets you encounter on your route is under construction, and you have to take a detour. Suddenly, you become much more aware and alert to all of your surroundings, perhaps even getting nervous and anxious about where to turn next. At this point, you are literally paying attention to whatever you can see in order to help guide and navigate you back to your original course of travel. Each turn and crossroad becomes a different landmark that you the driver start paying attention to so that you can become more cognizant of your current surroundings. Now, you have gone from auto-pilot to hands-on pilot.

For many of us who grew up without the benefit of Internet maps or GPS, this seems like a difficult and stressful situation to be in. Most technological devises can be counted on to simply guide you the driver back to your original comfort zones without having to try too hard. So why bother trying to pay attention to anything for such reasons, when the machine can do most of the work for you instead of using your brains? And for that question, I simply say that no matter what the situation calls for, the *mind* is always the most reliable weapon we have. No amount of power outages, internet interruptions, or lack of cell phone signals, will ever truly impair the intrinsic workings of the human brain. Sometimes just thinking about something can seem like just another "walk" through the park, or in this case, the palace.

However, one thing we did not talk about earlier was the question of how does one actually "walk" through a memory palace correctly, without really having to physically walk at all. As I said earlier, places that you currently or recently have seen will all be fresh in your mind, yet older places might be harder to visualize. Don't worry about looking up any information about the layout of such places, just use your best judgment as far as how you remembered the place actually looked. Next time you walk into a room of a building that you are familiar with, first take notice of the point of view or angle that you are seeing things through when you first arrive at the entrance door. Either the door will be to the left or right-side entrance to a room.

Try to make this your initial or "first" location in a room. After that, try to notice the next major thing about the room that attracts your eyes. This will be the "second" location in the room. It could be a piece of furniture, a picture, a window, or some other personal item. Then decide for yourself if you would like to "walk" through the room either clockwise or counter-clock wise. Do this for each and every major or large object that falls within that path, and number each location until you eventually return back to the door you started at. Try to use the same turn of direction for each room you walk through in your journeys. It will make it easier to remember what items are coming first and second, as opposed to changing direction each time you get to another room. You can use the same philosophy when it comes to getting over to the next room, depending on how your palace rooms are connected to each other

The next step to take is where the real test of memory truly begins. What you have to do now is to try to take whatever information you want to try to memorize, and mentally "insert" that information along the various locations of your memory palace. And in order to do this, you will have to visualize such information in great graphic detail, almost as if you were trying to purposely "hallucinate" the images right in front of you. Don't worry, just because I am a shrink does not mean I want you to think you are becoming purposely psychotic. However, the first item that you want to remember will have to be placed or inserted, next to the first location in one of your memory palaces. Then the second item that you want to memorize will have to be placed next to the second location in one of your memory palace, and so on.

In using the method of loci, when the person wants to remember several items in a row, the person mentally 'walks' through the different locations, or <u>loci</u>, in their imagination and then tries to connect each piece of information next to each separate location. This is done by forming a picture connecting the pieces of information to any features of the physical location in the room. This process works because what we are really doing, is to trying to<u> connect something that we do know (the journey location) to something else that we have yet to know (the new information)</u>. The ability to recall or retrieve this information is achieved by simply 'walking' through the journey once again, and as you go from one location to the next, you then "arrive" at the desired piece of information in our minds once you reach such location. Seems quite "elementary", wouldn't you say?

You will also notice that as you walk from one location to another, that there is always another piece of information to recall that has a different color, shape, texture or quality to it from the previous one. Perhaps the items to remember are things like a street lamp, magnifying glass, deerstalker hat, and tobacco pipe. Imagine walking down a pathway, and around each turn or bend, a new item "pops" up as you continue along your journey. Maybe you will imagine a large street lamp at the first location in your Memory palace, and then you might continue to walk through it and later see a large magnifying glass at the next location. As you continue to walk through your Memory palace, you will continue to encounter each and every piece of information that you want to remember, as you move from one location to another. Somehow your brain is forcing you to hold onto each and every piece of material set before you by having it organized along the various locations in your memory palace.

Congratulations, you have just taken your first fictional "journey" through a memory journey. Now, do this for each and every house that you are either very familiar with, or places that you have not seen in many years. It could be the houses of friends, relatives, neighbors, coworkers, or just total strangers. As long as you have been in their house at least a few times, you should have a pretty good idea of the general layout of most of the rooms. Remember the layout of the rooms compared to each other, decide where you want to start (usually this is going to be the farthest away point), and then proceed from room to room until you either leave the house or exit into another floor.

Make sure you keep track of each and every single location that catches your attention, including all doors, windows, furniture, hallways and staircases. Then once you are confident that you are "traveled" through your memory palace well enough, use the following diagram and list to help you remember the travel spots that you have seen along the way. Do this for each and every memory palace you wish to create. If you need to, try to keep a <u>notebook or a binder</u> for such purposes and then label each journey as a separate page. Include a physical diagram along with the written list of locations for each palace. Below is an example of one of my personal memory journeys which takes place in my living room of my house.

() TITLE OF MEMORY JOURNEY
(ex, your house, apartment, work, etc)

Location #	Description of location (what the location actually is, looks like, and what it means)
1st	TV set (on my left hand side of vision)
2nd	Couch (as I turn and look directly at it)
3rd	Coffee table (as I turn right to walk away from couch)
4th	Easy chair (as I turn straight and look ahead)
5th	China cabinet (as I start to turn right and move forward)
6th	Windows (as I straighten up and start walking back to door)
7th	Lamp (in my left field of vision)
8th	Stereo set (as I look toward the door)
9th	Piano set (leaving the room)
10th	Same as before

11th	Same as before
12th	Same as before
13th	Same as before
14th	Same as before

Earlier, I made a joke about trying to "hallucinate" an actual image into your head and placing it at a different location inside your memory palace. Well, believe it or, you don't have to be crazy in order to have a strong and realistic imagination. And that is one of the most important skills to have in order to be able to effectively utilize the Memory Palace technique. In order to better be able to utilize a memory palace effectively, there is an exercise that I would like to give you before we talk further about memory journeys. And this exercise involves using your imagination skills, or your ability to use your "**inner senses**".

As you already know, you have 5 active senses: **sight, smell, taste, touch, and hearing**. For now, I would like for you to picture the following image in your mind and to use your senses to describe everything about it that you can. This will help you to strengthen your inner imagination and to be better able to create images or pictures in your head much easier so that you can utilize such mnemonic devices more effectively. Although most adults are all well grounded in reality and have a hard time conjuring up such unrealistic images, it is essentially the ability to use your cognitive imagination that is vitally important for any future "detective" of memory to be able to remember information more effectively.

I tend to use the same imagination exercise for all of my new students of memory. For your first exercise in imagination, try to envision an elephant holding a delicious ice cream snack. Wow, that must sound absolutely crazy to you, and indeed it should be. No elephant would ever be caught dead holding an ice cream in reality, and we would barely see such a thing on television or in the movies. However, in order to be able to use the Memory palace technique efficiently, you are going to have to let go of all of your preconceived notions of reality, and try to let your imagination run wild. Sherlock used to explain to his partner John Watson that he always hated boredom and despised simple challenges in life. He was always looking for an excuse to push his mind to the limit and challenge his own mental faculties in one way or another. And what better way to get you started on such a journey, then to strengthen the muscles of our own imagination.

Now then, getting back to my previous example with the elephant and the ice cream cone, I want you to try to imagine how the ice cream must taste when you take it from the elephant and put it in your mouth. Is the ice cream cold, creamy, sugary, or warm? Now, try to imagine what it feels like when the ice cream is melting on your skin. Does the ice cream feel sticky, gooey, or wet and drippy? Then, try to think about how the ice cream smells when you take a sniff of it. Do you smell the flavors, the sprinkles, or the cone itself? Wow, it seems like I might be making you get a little bit hungry with such visualizations, as I am forcing you to really think about this one particular object. Just remember, an elephant never "forgets".

At this point, maybe we should now take a peek at the elephant instead of focusing on the ice cream cone. What can you tell about such animal? If you stood close to the elephant, how do you think its skin would feel if you touched it? Would the skin be hard, full of scales, dry, flaky, or coarse? What would the elephant sound like to you if he made a roar? Would it be loud, soft, high or low? Finally, what would the elephant smell like to you? Would he be clean and fresh, or dirty and stinky? Close your eyes, concentrate hard, and get this picture in your head. Do this exercise for at least one to two minutes and try not to get distracted by anything else around you. This process is called **imaging** in the field of memory. It helps to better recall information as though you are watching a cartoon in your head. At some point, this image will seem quite "powerful" to you once you start to really use your senses.

I think it would be important to explain to you now about the **powers of imagination** and how they can help you to achieve an ultimate memory. Most of us are familiar with old fables and myths such as Santa Claus, the Bogeyman, the Tooth Fairy and the Easter Bunny. Though we are sure that we never truly met them in real life, most of us as children were very capable of imagining what these make-believe characters truly looked like, if only in our own minds. And these characters were much easier to create during our early imaginative years as opposed to us now as adults. But don't worry, even back in those days, having an imagination as strong as that was the key to remembering information more clearly than we do today. It seems as though every child under the age of 6 years of age had more eidetic memory than most adults do.

As times goes on, the ability to conjure up such ridiculous images seems to fade more and more from our adult minds, as we are constantly inundated with the harsh realities of life. We become less fulfilled with the carefree and relaxed feelings of our early childhood, and become more grounded in our current sense of reality. The important point to remember here is that the stronger or more powerful you make your imagination, the better you will be able to recall something through memory exercises. Hence, it is no different in terms of the actual amount of information to remember, it is only different in your mind as far as how graphic you make the images for such purposes.

Think of it like this, would you be better able to remember something that seemed boring and familiar, or something that was **outlandish** and **unexpected?** Chances are, you would be better able to remember the latter item as opposed to the first one. That is the reason for the previous story of the elephant with the ice cream. Our minds seem to crave stimulation and complexity. This is the reason that we only remember the good and bad days of our lives, never the boring days in between. For this purpose, you will need to be able to use your imagination to make sure that your future characters are engaged in wild and graphically crazy activities in order to visualize them longer and more clearly.

The phrase I chose to use to remember when creating such images goes like this: **POP**. This stands for two things, first it stands for **p**erson, **o**bject or **p**lace. Second, it actually means the word **POP**. (imagine popcorn bursting in your face) When you try to come up with different images in your mind, it is important to have your **POP (person, object, or place)** literally POP right in front of your face through the inner senses of your mind. This means that you have to try to imagine things happening amongst your imaginary characters that could never truly happen in your imagination or the real world. As difficult as this seems, it allows you to somehow abandon abstract reasoning and logical thought, and instead delve deep into the world of creative and illustrative thinking. It will be easier for you to remember these informational images as if they were engaged in some type of activity, or with some type of object, that seems out of place for them.

Now that we have already talked about the Memory palace technique and how to better use your imagination, let's touch upon the second major technique of cognitive enhancement. And this technique is usually called **the LINK METHOD,**. For most of us, the image of a link is usually very easy to conjure up. A chain is usually a series of "links" connected together into one large ongoing form. If one link breaks or falls apart, the rest of the chain is worthless. Memory behaves in the same way. If you can get one piece of information to be linked or connected to another piece of information, and again for another piece of information, then you are creating your very own "chain of memories". And by doing this, you make it so much easier to be able to recall or remember information simply by thinking of the first piece of information in a particular sequence, as seen below.

CHAIN	LINK	CHAIN	LINK

When we were all younger, a lot of us were familiar with a special game referred to as dominoes. I know from my own experience, that I used to love stacking dominoes one in front of the other in a straight pattern. And then, when I was finished placing all of the dominoes, my favorite part was tipping over one domino and watching it hit the next one, and then the next one. I would continue to watch until all of the dominoes had toppled over on the floor. And none of this would have been possible without the dominoes all being close to or linked next to each other, and then just knocking over the first one at the beginning of the sequence.

This method, although slightly slower and more time consuming than the Memory Palace technique, is still just as effective in memorizing information, especially information that is organized in sequential order. The way it works is like this; you take one piece of information that you want to memorize, and you find a way to associate it, or "link" it to another piece of information that you already know from before. In this respect, you are connecting both pieces of information to each other.

For example, when I think of Sherlock Holmes, I immediately conjure up images of a deerstalker hat, a magnifying class, a trench coat, and a calabash pipe, just to name a few.

All of these different images are things that most people usually associate with the legendary fictional detective himself. In this respect, I am taking one initial piece of information (Sherlock), and then trying to associate various pieces of other information (hat, magnifying glass, coat, pipe) to such person. Much like the example I gave earlier about the dominoes falling down, when most of us think about Sherlock Holmes, it does not take long to imagine at least several different associated images or artifacts related to such person, one after another.

Another way to try to delineate the concept of the Link or Chain Method is to use a procedure that is quite familiar in the memory world, known as "setting the stage", or the **PAO method**. PAO stands for **PERSON-ACTION-OBJECT**. When you think about the word "**link**", it should conjure up an image of either a chain or a rope that is able to connect or "**link**" two items together so that they are connected to each other. The setting the scene sequence is the very same concept described here. In this instance, you should be able to make connections between any two unrelated and dissimilar entities or objects in such the same way as you would by linking them together.

In this respect, you would try to imagine one major object having some type of interaction or "effect" upon another object right next to it. The first object to remember would be in the viewer's internal field of vision on their left-hand side or pictured as occurring on the far-left side of the particular memory location (loci) they are using. Then the second object would be remembered in the viewer's right-hand side, or just right next to the first object. This type of "domino effect" of one thing having an effect on another is pretty much self-evident and without exception, because as Sherlock would state "An exception can only disprove the rule".

PERSON (1)	**ACTION (2)**	**OBJECT (3)**

When you think about it, this particular process just seems to make sense in terms of the laws of physics or cause and effects. Normally, a person would engage in some type of action, and this type of action would have a particular effect on another person or object next to them. This domino effect of one thing effecting another is the gold standard for making memories <u>stick or link together</u>. We are all aware that there is such a thing known as gravity, so think of it as what goes up will always come down. Or, if you want to get more technical, every action has an equal or opposite reaction. This lets your mind always realize that the first item in a list of other items ultimately has an effect on the rest of the items. This almost sounds poetic in of itself.

I know all of this does not sound easy to understand. In order to better illustrate such example to you, let's try to use our imagination for just a brief moment. Try to imagine an actor on a stage, reciting Shakespeare to the crowded audience. You are in the front row watching this person perform. Now, try to picture such person standing on the far-left side of the stage from *your* vantage point, or POV. This "person" is gesturing (action) sideways with their arm, and then talking to a fictional "object" on the right side of the stage, and this object represents something personal to the actor. In this instance, you could substitute a set of images to <u>represent the person,</u> and then another set of images to represent the actual <u>action of gesturing</u>, and another set of images to represent the <u>fictional object </u>on the far right side of the stage.

As we have all normally been trained to read a sentence in a book starting from left to right, we can do much the same thing when we are trying to memorize items using the PAO method. The *Shakespearian actor* is set to the far left of the scene as he represents the first item to be memorized, and the actor's arm is *physically gesturing* to the next object on his right. This would be the second piece of information to remember. The *object* on the far right of the stage would represent the third piece of information to remember. And in the end, you have the essential elements of the PAO system.

Just in case this seems to be somewhat difficult to conceptualize, let me give you one last illustrative example. Let's try to imagine our brilliant friend Sherlock Holmes is standing over his desk and looking through his magnifying glass, as he is examining a pile of random pieces of paper. In this instance, you could imagine Sherlock Holmes standing in your left field of vision, or on your left hand side. Try to imagine him hunched over while facing towards your right hand side, or your right field of vision. Next, try to picture him looking through his magnifying glass while hunched over.

Lastly, now try to imagine that he is hunched over a desk, looking down at a pile of papers scattered across such desk. This is located in your right POV, or point of view. In this respect, you are utilizing the very same principles that were set before you in the previous paragraphs. You are imagining the person (Sherlock Holmes), the action (looking through magnifying glass), and the object (piles of papers). And you are doing this activity while going from left to right, in a straight forward or *linking* sequence.

SHERLOCK HOLMES	LOOKING THROUGH GLASS	PILE OF PAPERS

In terms of trying to use this particular concept or method in regards to the Memory Palace technique, what you could do is try to imagine such a sequence of items occurring at each and every location or loci in one of your Memory Palaces. In this respect, what you are doing is creating a small and unusual storyline at each location in each room of your respective palace. Then you would be simply walking through such palace and encountering each individual storyline as you navigate through.

So, let's try to imagine that you are in one of the rooms of your respective memory palace, and the first thing that you encounter is a Shakespearean actor in your left field of vision. You notice that such actor is gesturing with his arm, towards your right field of vision, or your right side. And in his arm, he is holding a skull high in the air. So in this respect, you are first going to notice the actor (person) in your left point of view. Then notice the action that he is engaging in (gesturing with his hand), and then finally noticing the object that is of importance to him (skull) in your right point of view.

And then after you have seen this particular scene in front of you, you move onwards towards the next location in your memory palace. And at this location, you spot Sherlock Holmes, and he is facing forwards towards your right hand side. And he is looking downwards through his magnifying glass at a stack of papers on his desk counter. At this location, you are noticing the person (Sherlock), the action (glancing through glass), and the object (pile of papers), going from left to right.

There you have it; you have just used the link method, or the PAO method, to remember random pieces of information in sequential order throughout various locations in your memory palace. And each item that you were memorizing, whether it is the person, action or object, each item should have a special meaning to you. Try to imagine that the person that you are memorizing represents something else. Now try to imagine that the action you are memorizing represents something else.

And finally, try to imagine that the object at the end of the sequence represents something else. I know that this particular concept feels somewhat confusing to you; however I will discuss such topic with you next. But don't worry, as we get further into the book, we will talk more about how to link, organize, and code information that is supposed to be memorized. Because in the end, there is no greater "substitute" than this.

And finally, now that we have talked about the Memory Palace Method, and the Link or Chain Method, as well as the PAO method, let's end this chapter by talking about the last major method of memorizing information; and that method is called the **Substitution Method**. This method is basically the core process in coding information when it comes to being used in memorization. In this respect, what we are actually doing is trying to "change" the information that we want to memorize, and making it look or sound different than it already is. In laymen's terms, we are trying to take the material that we are attempting to memorize, and "substituting" another image in its place, so that we can more easily store such information in our Memory Palaces for later recall.

Before you start to think that this method is beyond your capabilities, let's try to ask ourselves some questions about certain phrases that we are used to using in our daily lives. Most of us are familiar with expressions such as "that reminds me of", or "that seems familiar", or simply having moments of déjà vu. To be honest, not all information that you want to memorize can be visually processed or delineated in your head exactly as you see it. Sometimes you have to take such information and try to change what it looks or sounds like, in order to make it seem more familiar to you. And in this case, you will have to use your imagination as well as your own personal inventory of mnemonic "codes" for such purposes.

Going back on the example of the elephant with the ice cream cone, let's try to re-imagine such scenario in our heads again. Try to imagine the elephant is standing in your left field of vision, and he is actively using his tongue to lick an ice cream cone, which is dripping all over the floor on your right hand side. While this might seem somewhat familiar in regards to the <u>LINK or PAO method</u>, how about we try to change things up a little bit? Suppose you are trying to imagine a large brain. And this large brain is located on your left hand side of vision. Now, imagine this large brain has tiny arms, and it is playing an electric guitar. And while this large brain is playing an electric guitar, imagine the musical notes are floating towards your right hand side of vision, and such notes are landing into a large basket full of birds.

Wow, I bet all of you out there are scratching your heads, wondering if this writer has suddenly "lost his mind". Well, don't worry, I assure you that what I just described, makes perfect sense to me. And it will make perfect sense to you once I begin to explain where this particular imaginary sequence came from. Earlier, I asked you to remember the images of an elephant licking an ice cream cone. And then I asked you to remember the images of a large brain playing a guitar, while musical notes are flowing out of it, and landing in a basket full of birds. And, you were asked to memorize such information in a left to right sequence. Now, while you may think that both sets of images are entirely different, let me explain how both sets of images are actually very much the same.

When using the **Substitution Method**, what you are really doing is trying to "substitute" one image to be related to another image in your mind. In this respect, when I was thinking about the elephant, the first thing that came to my mind was the old adage about "elephants never forget". And in this respect, this made me think of a large brain. Then, I had to figure out a way to remember the actual act of licking ice cream. And for this, I chose to imagine the brain physically playing an electric guitar. Without giving out particular names, I used to be a fan of the rock band "KISS" when I was a child, and I usually imagine a large tongue when I think of such a band.

Finally, when it came to trying to remember the ice cream cone, I simply remembered that I used to like to go out to eat ice cream at Baskin Robbins when I was a child. I also remembered that I used to mispronounce the name of such company, as I would often call it "Basket Robbins". So with that, I instantly picture a "basket" full of "robins". And there you have it, I have used the Substitution Method to remember different pieces of information by "substituting" different images to be associated with such mnemonic information.

LARGE TONGUE	EQUALS	KISS BAND

While this might seem like quite an unusual and uncomfortable form of memorization, I assure you that the only two things that you really need to use are your *imagination* and your *own personal preferences*. Let me explain what I mean by when I say *personal preferences*, or life experiences. Each of us has led a different life from each other, and each of us has various things that we have encountered in our daily lives that have stayed with us in our minds. Whether it be characters from your favorite movies, books, TV shows, plays, or whether it be actual real people or places in your life, each one of us has a long storyline of countless items in our lives that were very sentimental to us.

And the only thing that you have to do is to use your imagination and try to visualize such images in your mind whenever you want to try to remember associated pieces of information. Whether it be each time you think of a deerstalker hat, a magnifying glass, or a crime scene, you can easily try to remember something personal and specific from your own life that can be somehow connected with such images.

And like that, you have now learned three different mnemonic techniques that can be used for any type of memorization task set before you. Also, what you may not have realized is that all three of these memorization techniques are actually able to be used **together at the very same time**. This makes the task of memorization almost completely full-proof in that you can never truly fail at any attempt to remember information. This is the perfect trifecta of cognitive related tools and techniques to be used in our daily lives. However, in order to better understand how these methods work together, it is important to understand the inherent relationship between all three of them

Let me try to explain how to use all three methods together in a simple way. First, try to make sure that you already have a certain number of different Memory Palaces already picked out and outlined for your own personal references. Second, when you are moving throughout your respective Memory Palaces, always try to "link" your new information to any of the various objects or loci which are located throughout such Memory Palaces. And third, if the information that you want to memorize is difficult to imagine or picture in your head, simply use the Substitution Method, by creating a similar image in your mind that can be associated with what you were attempting to memorize in the first place. And from there, you are guaranteed to be able to memorize any list of information that is presented in front of you with nearly perfect recall.

At this point, I have now taught you all of the specific skills and techniques that can be used in regards to memorizing information that is set before you. You should try to take the time to practice moving around through all of your various Memory Palaces so that you get familiar with them. In addition, you should try to use your imagination strongly, and always do your best to graphically picture whatever information you want to try to attach to different loci within your palaces. And finally, be willing to try to substitute various words and symbols when it comes to memorizing information that is difficult to conceptualize. This way you are capable of always having some type of coding system for whatever information is out there to be memorized.

For the rest of this book, I will be teaching you how to memorize DIFFERENT types of information in different subjects. I will briefly go over how to use each of the three major mnemonic devices that were set before you. And then, I will be giving some practice quizzes and homework for you to do for each chapter. This way you can be able to run through how best to memorize each and every type of material that is presented to you. So try to do your best to get comfortable and familiar with these different "techniques", or as Sherlock would call them "you know my methods". We are going to delve into the first subject of memorization: **NUMBERS MEMORY**.

CHAPTER 3

DOMINIC MNOMENIC (NUMBERS MEMORY)

Several years ago, I remember watching an episode of a different TV series based upon the legendary detective Sherlock Holmes. However, this series not only featured different actors and actresses, but also was the only type of TV series that portrayed Sherlock Holmes in modern day times. In this new series, the main characters are set in modern day, 21st century England; however the story lines are extremely similar to the short stories written by Arthur Conan Doyle many years ago. And, some of the titles of the stories had been changed or edited as well, yet the storylines remain similar.

In one episode, entitled "A Scandal in Belgravia", there is one scene where Sherlock Holmes is examining a secret message which has been inconspicuously given to him by his femme fatale nemesis, Irene Adler. In this encoded message, there are a series of numbers and letters mixed together to form a certain message. During such time, John Watson is busy researching information while sitting near his laptop computer. Secretly, Irene Adler already knows the main subject pertaining to this particular numerical enigma; yet she wants to see if Sherlock Holmes can make sense of it himself, as she is planning to use such information for her own nefarious purposes.

In that one instant, as she is about to plant a seductive kiss on the cheek of Sherlock, he quickly examines the series of numbers, memorizes them, and begins to encrypt the hidden message behind the unrelated series of random digits. And in just a few seconds, he is able to determine that this "secret" message of numbers is in fact information relating to the seat arrangements on board a specific airplane that is about to take off in the next day or so. Irene is so astonished and amazed by this dazzling display of mnemonic superiority that she passionately flirts with Sherlock and promises to include him in her master plan.

Now for most of us, the idea of being able to look at a series of numbers and then try to remember the exact order and sequence of such digits seems like an unbelievable feat that only the great Sherlock Holmes would be capable of. However, the ability to successfully memorize numbers and their numerical values is really not that difficult to achieve once you start to learn some of the lessons that I am about to give you in this chapter. In order to begin to understand the science and methodology behind memorizing numbers, let's first start at the beginning by trying to define what a <u>number</u> actually is.

A **number** is a mathematical object used to count, measure, and label information. More universally, individual numbers can be represented by <u>symbols</u>, called *numerals*. For example, "5" is a numeral that represents the actual number of "five". Basic numerals are usually organized in a certain numerical system, which is a structured classification designed to physically represent any number. The most common numeral system currently used today is the type that allows for the representation of any number by using a combination of one of only ten fundamental symbols, called <u>digits</u> (0,1,2,3, up until 9). In addition to their use in counting items and measuring dimensions, numerals are often used for markers such as telephone numbers, birthdays, and historical dates.

Numbers are a part of all aspects of our lives, regardless of how we feel about them. In addition to things like your phone number, social security information, bank accounts, birthdates, and historical information, numbers can be found in almost all facets of our lives. Addresses, times of day, zip codes and medical coding, are all forms of information where numbers play a huge part. Some people might argue that numbers play just as much a part of our daily lives as actual letters, but that subject is up for debate. For now, let's try to focus on only what numbers essentially are, not how are they actually used in our daily lives.

It has been argued that, in relation to other pieces of visual information, numbers in of themselves are considered arbitrary and ambiguous in nature. For centuries, the actual symbols of numerical values have changed over the course of history, without changing the inherent value of such integers. Whether it is hieroglyphic symbolism, Roman numerals, or mathematic constants, the physical representation of numerical values continues to change based upon the intended usage of such information. This is not to say that letters have not changed throughout the course of history. It is just that most people have never truly realized that numbers are just as arbitrary and ambiguous in their own lives as the letters of the alphabet.

However, due to the fact that the symbols of numbers have physically changed throughout the years as well as their inherent usage, this allows us to be able to remember numbers in whatever shape or form we wish to. Whether it is memorizing a telephone number, a computer code, or just remembering important financial information, most of the actual symbols for numbers are the same as the ones that we are used to seeing on our cell phones and computer keyboards. And since we are all familiar with how numerical digits physically look, we can try to use some of the previously mentioned mnemonic devices in order to better memorize them. To give you a better example of what I am talking about, I have included two lists of the **10 actual numerical digits** that are used in modern day society, along with two different ways to memorize them. (sight + sound, remember the <u>substitution method</u>?)

0 = zero	**(picture a hole)**
1 = one	**(picture a fishing pole)**
2 = two	**(picture a picture hanger)**
3 = three	**(picture a harp sideways)**
4 = four	**(picture a hatchet)**
5 = five	**(picture a large fishing hook)**
6 = six	**(picture a golf club)**
7 = seven	**(picture a measuring level)**
8 = eight	**(picture the symbol for infinity)**
9 = nine	**(picture a backwards "e")**

0 = **zero**	**(sounds like Zorro)**
1 = **one**	**(sounds like gun)**
2 = **two**	**(sounds like shoe)**
3 = **three**	**(sounds like knee)**
4 = **four**	**(sounds like door)**
5 = **five**	**(sounds like hive)**
6 = **six**	**(sounds like sticks)**
7 = **seven**	**(sounds like heaven)**
8 = **eight**	**(sounds like gate)**
9 = **nine**	**(sounds like wine)**

As most of you remember from the previous chapter in this book, the Substitution Method is where you try to substitute information that you already know, to be associated with information that you don't already know. In this instance, you can decide to look at a number and determine not only what you think the actual number "looks" like, but also what it "sounds" like. As you can see, I have included two lists of the way that I myself chose to memorize numbers using the Substitution Method.

Don't assume that you have to use the actual symbols and images that I have already listed; this is just an example of something that I came up with a few years ago. But the science behind it makes sense, as you are trying to look and listen to a number and then link such number together with information that makes the most sense to you. (remember the previous story about using your inner senses). However, before you start to think that there is only one way to actually memorize numbers, let me introduce you to 2 different methods for actually encoding numbers so as to be able to eventually memorize them.

The most common and oldest mnemonic system that is used in the field of memorization for numbers is referred to as the **Major Mnemonic**. This type of number memory system was first utilized at least two hundred years ago. The major mnemonic is a system where the person works by converting numbers into consonant sounds, and then converting them back into words by adding vowels in between. As you remember from school, vowels are the letters (**A, E, I, O, U**).

This is referred to as the fill-in, or the information that you fill-in for the number that you are memorizing in order to make it an actual word.

In this system, you will have to be able to vocally pronounce certain sounds or words and be able to recall the sounds acoustically in your memory so that you can create mental images. In the table below, the consonant sounds are listed; however you will more than likely have to try to pronounce the various sounds over and over in order to become more familiar with how it feels to say them out loud. Each numeral is associated with one or more consonants so that you have more than one choice. Vowels and the consonants *w*, *h*, and *y* are ignored for this purpose.

The Major Mnemonic system is organized like this, as I have included a table below to outline what the system looks likes.

Numeral	Sounds	Commonly associated letters
0	/s/, /z/	s, soft *c*, z, x (in *xylophone*)
1	/t/, /d/	t, d
2	/n/	N
3	/m/	M
4	/r/	r, l (in *colonel*)
5	/l/	L
6	/ c h / , /g/ /sh/,	ch (in *cheese* and *chef*), j, soft g, sh, c (in *cello* and *special*), and *vision*), sc (in *fascist*), sch (in *schwa* and *eschew*)
7	/k/, /g/	k, hard c, q, ch (in *loch*), hard g
8	/f/, /v/	f, ph (in *phone*), v, gh (in *laugh*)
9	/p/, /b/	p, b, gh (in *cough*)

As you can see, each number is connected to a certain set of sounds and pronunciations, as well as tongue positions. In regards to this technique, the most important thing to remember is the actual phonetic sound that is made by the word itself. That is to say, it is the consonant sounds that matter most in this particular technique, not the actual spelling of the word. You will have to probably write down different words for different combinations of letters that sound easy enough for you to not only pronounce, but also to visually imagine in your head.

Therefore, a word like *"action"* would look (or sound) like the numbers *762*, as you can see from the future phonetic spelling (/k/-/sh/-/n/), not *712* (*k-t-n*). Double letters are disregarded when they are not pronounced separately, such as the word *muddy* sounds like *31* (/m/-/d/), not *311*, however the word *midday* would be like *311* (/m/-/d/-/d/). This takes some time and practice in order to learn, it is the most complicated and advanced mnemonic learning system out there. However it has been proven to be extremely effective in memorizing numbers and letters and cards at almost supernatural speeds. In this system, what we are really doing is trying to convert numbers to letters and then sounds. For most of us, this seems like an odd thing to do. We all grew up learning the alphabet as children as well as our numbers. Now, here we are trying to actually connect both systems of learning to each other.

However, before you start getting confused, don't worry too much about having to use this particular method. I just want to reiterate that, although I am familiar with this particular type of mnemonic system, my main goal here in this book is to teach you a **different yet similar system of memory**. All I wanted to do was *introduce* you to the Major Mnemonic system, whether or not you chose to use it is based upon your own preferences. Many world famous and internally renowned memory champions are fluent with such system when it comes to remembering numbers. However this system can take an extraordinary amount of time and energy to learn. For now, I have become very familiar with a different type of numbers memory system, which as it turns out was only invented a few decades ago. And that particular mnemonic technique is called the **Dominic System**.

The **Dominic system** is a mnemonic system used to remember sequences of digits similar to the mnemonic major system. It was invented and used in competition by eight-time World Memory Champion <u>Dominic O'Brien</u>. I should point out that the main difference between the Dominic system and the <u>Major system</u> is the assignment of *sounds and letters* to actually physical digits. The Dominic system is actually <u>a letter-based abbreviation</u> system where the letters comprise the initials of someone's name, while the major system is typically used as a <u>phonetic-based consonant</u> sounding system for objects, animals, persons, or even words.

In other words, using the Dominic system, one could create words or images for numbers using initials or abbreviations to stand for something dimensional in their minds rather than remembering corresponding sounds for such purposes. I also would like to point out that as an author on the subject of memory improvement, **I DO NOT CLAIM TO HAVE ANY RIGHTS, OWNERSHIP, OR PROPRIETORSHIP** of the actual Dominic Mnemonic, as it was invented by Mr. Dominic O'Brien. The actual chart or legend (if you are familiar with maps), is included below in order to help you the reader to understand how the Dominic system is organized.

Number	1	2	3	4	5	6	7	8	9	0
Letter	A	B	C	D	E	S	G	H	N	O

At first, this system seems to make sense when you count from the numbers 0-5, as we all are familiar with the alphabet. For instance, O can look like or be associated with the number 0. The letter A is the first letter of the alphabet, corresponding to the number 1, the letter B is associated with two, and so on. However, when we get to <u>6</u>, the corresponding letter turns out to be the <u>letter S</u>. And for the <u>number 9</u>, the corresponding letter happens to be the <u>letter N</u>. For many of us, this can stop us dead in our tracks, as we begin to mentally go over the alphabet in our heads and realize that the sixth letter of the alphabet turns out to be the letter <u>F</u>, and the ninth letter of the alphabet happens to be the letter <u>I</u>.

In order to better explain this particular diagram, Dominic O'Brien has decided that it would be easier for the student of memory to only use these precise letters, as it appears to make it easier to come up with abbreviations and initials for such purposes. For this particular formula, the word "**six**" actually starts with the letter **S**, and the word "**nine**" actually starts with the letter **N**. The reason we chose to do this is because for most people it seems far easier to imagine various characters and caricatures using only the associated letters as described.

However, if you chose to create your own method of memory training, and wish to use the letters F and N, then please be my guest. The best thing about this particular method of memory training is that there is no one right or wrong way to connect letters and numbers. It is entirely within the discretion of the user to determine what connections and associations such person choses to use. The only thing that is important is that such system makes sense to the individual person's needs.

Also, if you ever wanted to memorize just <u>single digits or numbers</u>, simply just use the Dominic systems already mentioned and then try to create different images for each individual number. For example, in the Dominic System, the number **01** is equal to letter **A**. So, I could think of something special in my life that has the letter A in it, such as an <u>apple</u>. For the number **02**, the equivalent letter for such number is **B**, so I could think of something in my life that also starts with the letter B, such as a <u>banana</u>. You can easily think of a few other images to correspond to the remaining numbers between 0-9 in your own time. By doing this, you can make room for the possibility of being able to memorize an odd amount of information, or just simply memorizing numbers one digit at a time (though this may take longer, some people are okay with such method).

However, if you really want to utilize the system of the Dominic Mnemonic in a more expeditious manner, I have always found that you should try to memorize not one, but rather TWO numbers at the same time. The reasons why I say this is because, when it comes to creating images in your head that are unique and special, sometimes the best way to ignite your imaginative abilities, are to think of two numbers as being not simply a two digit number, but rather "initials" or an "abbreviation". This set of initials or abbreviations can be delineated or associated with a random mental image that you can create. In other words, one pair of numbers can equal one actual character or a complex image.

There is a big difference between the Major Mnemonic and the Dominic System. In going back on the previous subject of the Major Mnemonic, in this memory system, the *sounds* of T + L are assigned to the number 15, and then the person would have to find a word that has the same sounds as the first two consonants. Mnemonic images such as "tiles" or "toolbox" could be assigned under the major system using the number 15. However, in the Dominic system, the number 15 would actually stand for the letters **A** and **E**, and these letters could be used as the initials of someone's name—for example, **A**lbert **E**instein. Albert Einstein would then be given a **characteristic action**, such as "writing on a blackboard". Each two-digit number between 00 and 99 would have its own corresponding "person" as well as its associated and distinctive action.

As you can probably guess, the only numbers that you will have to create images for are the numbers from 00-99, which equals 100. The idea behind this is to sit down and make up a list of at least **100 different famous or fictional people** whose initials correspond to the associated numbers connected to those initials. Each person, or character you create, must be different and unique from the previous one. This means that each "character" needs to have their own trademark or distinguishing characteristic that sets them apart from others. In this instance, the person using the Dominic system would only have to write out a list for each number from 00-99, and determine what letters correspond to each set of numbers. And then that person would later have to decide upon a name for each person or character whose initials match that related set of letters.

In order to perform the encoding of numbers to letters correctly, each digit (00-99) needs to be linked or associated with letters using the table marked previously. These letters then become the initials of the person or character representing that number. Once the coding for a pair of digits is in place, a future linkage of digits can be changed into a story. This is done by first encoding one pair of digits as a **person**, and then another pair of digits to resemble an **action,** or **object**, and then chaining this person and action or object together in a small story.

This was a subject we covered earlier called the **PAO system of memorization**) The first object to remember would appear in the viewer's internal field of vision on their left-hand side or pictured as occurring on the left side of the particular memory location (loci) they are using. Then the second object would be remembered in the viewer's <u>right-hand side</u>, or just on the <u>right side</u> of the person's view, and so on.

Below is a scale that I created that helped me out when I had to come up with ideas for the **100 different characters or persons** that I could use as references for my various codes or numbers. The columns are listed in a way that makes it easier for the person to organize their materials and to see how each set of numbers can be linked to each pair of letters. By this I mean, you will need to come up with **exactly 100 different characters or images** that you can think of that relate to the corresponding letter codes for each number (***this will be the single most important assignment to complete on your own before moving on with this book, so please take your time and work on this first***). In order to do this correctly, you will have to create a numbered list going from 00-99, using the same format and organization as I have previously mentioned. The reference guide is listed below as follows:

NUMBER	INITIALS	NAME (person or character)	ACTION (what action most relates to them)	OBJECT (what object most relates to them)
00	OO	Whoever/whatever	Action or sequence	Object or item
01	OA	Whoever/whatever	Action or sequence	Object or item
02	OB	Whoever/whatever	Action or sequence	Object or item
03	OC	Whoever/whatever	Action or sequence	Object or item
04	OD	Whoever/whatever	Action or sequence	Object or item
05	OE	Whoever/whatever	Action or sequence	Object or item
06-100	Use Dominic Codes	Same	same	same

This process will take some time; don't be in a hurry to get the list done too quickly. The best advice I can give you when it comes to creating your characters is to simply use your "**inner instinct**". That is to say, when you first write down the initials that are associated with the corresponding numbers, ask yourself what is the very first thing you think of when you see or hear the letters. It has to be something that takes less than a few seconds to come up to your mind, something that feels natural or just makes sense to you. Always trust your instincts, as these things often take the least amount of mental energy to create. If the image is not too easy to conjure up, simply try to think of something else that is reasonably easy to picture. I have enclosed a reference chart for your convenience. This will be used by you in order to come up with codes for all of your related number memory tasks. Without these essential building blocks, memorizing numbers would be impossible, as you would not have the necessary ingredients. Or as Sherlock would say, "I cannot make bricks without clay"

EXAMPLE OF NUMBER CODING CHART FOR DOMINIC SYSTEM:

NUMBERS	LETTERS	NUMBERS	LETTERS
00	OO	51	EA
01	OA	52	EB
02	OB	53	EC
03	OC	54	ED
04	OD	55	EE
05	OE	56	ES
06	OS	57	EG
07	OG	58	EH
08	OH	59	EN
09	ON	60	SO
10	AO	61	SA
11	AA	62	SB
12	AB	63	SC
13	AC	64	SD
14	AD	65	SE
15	AE	66	SS
16	AS	67	SG
17	AG	68	SH
18	AH	69	SN
19	AN	70	GO
20	BO	71	GA
21	BA	72	GB

22	BB	73	GC
23	BC	74	GD
24	BD	75	GE
25	BE	76	GS
26	BS	77	GG
27	BG	78	GH
28	BH	79	GN
29	BN	80	HO
30	CO	81	HA
31	CA	82	HB
32	CB	83	HC
33	CC	84	HD
34	CD	85	HE
35	CE	86	HS
36	CS	87	HG
37	CG	88	HH
38	CH	89	HN
39	CN	90	NO
40	DO	91	NA
41	DA	92	NB
42	DB	93	NC
43	DC	94	ND
44	DD	95	NE
45	DE	96	NS
46	DS	97	NG
47	DG	98	NH
48	DH	99	NN
49	DN		
50	EO		

For this scale, when I see the number **68**, I already think of the letters **SH**. Here, I "instinctively" think of **S**herlock **H**olmes, since those are his initials. And from there, I can easily picture our famed detective in whatever shape or form I wish. However, this does not always work for every single combination of letters. You will sometimes not be able to go with your instincts for certain letters, as some combinations of letters are difficult to imagine any related characters for.

So please use your best judgment and decide what character or person you are most comfortable with using for each combination of letters. Try to make sure that each character is someone different or unique from the others. The more closely similar two characters are, the greater the chance that when you start memorizing long strings of information, you might confuse one combination of characters for another. Also, don't forget that the more outrageous or unique the character is, the better the chance you will never forget it or confuse it with anything else.

As I mentioned, sometimes if you have two characters that are similar in nature, there is a greater chance that you might get confused later on when you are trying to memorize information. For instance, the number **26** can be translated as **BS**. And BS could possibly stand for "**B**aker **S**treet", which as you remember is the address for Sherlock Holmes. Now, unless of course I can come up with a very peculiar symbol which could designate something similar to the physical address of Sherlock Holmes, there is a great chance that if I tried to memorize both the numbers **68** and **26** together, I might get confused. This is because it might be hard for me to effectively separate both terms in my head as distinct and separate units of information. In this respect, what I am trying to do is memorize 4 numbers together as one single unit; therefore it helps if each pair of numbers has a different quality from each other.

Four numbers, or the pairing of two sets of numbers, have a fundamental purpose in the field of numerical memory. As you recall from my previous description, when you created your own memory palaces, you could either draw a picture of each room on a sheet of paper, or you could create a numerical list of all the different points of reference. By doing either of these things, you now have the ability to organize your materials in a more realistic way. The next step is to actually know <u>how much information</u> you want to store at each location.

Earlier, in the activity known as "setting the scene", you were told to imagine a character on the left side of a stage, pointing to someone or something else on the right side of the stage. The first character represented the first 2 numbers, and the other character represented the next 2 numbers. If you were to imagine such a scenario playing out at any one of your locations within your memory palace, you would have the ability to easily remember an average of at <u>least 4 numbers</u> for each location.

The only thing you have to remember is to place the first item in your left field of vision and the other image in your right field of vision. (if you become really good at this, you could probably double that amount per each location if you have enough space). This allows you to always know that the amount of information that you can remember at each location will be 2, 4, 6, or 8 digits long, depending on how many images you can put at each loci. It is best to always stick with the same number of characters for each location, as well as the same amount of numerical digits, so that you don't get bogged down by the math. (I always hated division growing up)

When I chose to memorize numbers, I am able to put <u>2 different characters in each location</u> standing right next to each other, thereby allowing me to get 4 digits of numbers per location. And when I do this, I make up a short story or "play" for how all the characters and objects interact. This allows me to have better control over the mathematical calculations needed to recall where the 10th, 20th, or 30th digit would be located. All I have to do count each location as either being the first, second or third location, and then just <u>multiply that number by four.</u> This lets me know what group of numbers corresponds to which specific location.

For example, if I wanted to memorize 40 different numbers, it would take me at least 10 different locations in order to fit all of such information in it. If I wanted to recall what the 27th number in the sequence was, I would realize that the first location in my memory palace could only be used for the first four numbers. And then the second location could be used for the next four numbers and so on. (i.e. Location one (**#1-4**), location two (**#5-8**), location three (**#9-12**). Therefore, it is easy to realize that the 27th number would be located in the 7th location in your memory palace, as this location could encompass the 25th to 28th digits in the sequence. In this order, the 27th number would be <u>the first initial</u> of the <u>second character</u> on the <u>right hand side</u> of <u>location 7.</u> I have enclosed another chart underneath to show you how it is organized. Try using this as a reference guide for those of you who have already completed your palaces. It refers to the previous memory journey list that was used for my living room.

(#) TITLE OF MEMORY JOURNEY
(ex, your house, apartment, work)

Location #	Description of location (include what the location actually is and what it means)
1st	TV set (items #1-4)
2nd	Couch (items #5-8)
3rd	Coffee table (items #9-12)
4th	Easy chair (items #13-16)
5th	China set cabinet (items #17-20)
6th	window (items #21-24)
7th	Lamp (items #25-28)
8th	Stereo location (items #29-32)
9th	Piano (items #33-36)
10th	Door leading out (items #37-40)

Now then, what do you say we stop talking about the mechanics and science behind memorizing numbers, and <u>actually try to memorize some real numbers for practice purposes?</u> I have included a list of at least **40 different numbers**, grouped together in pairs of two digits, each one next to each other. You will need two pieces of paper for this activity. In order to do this exercise correctly, what you will need to do is to write out the actual sequence of numbers on a scrap piece of paper. Then, after you have finished writing out the numbers as written in the book, flip this piece of paper over so that you cannot see them. Then, grab a second sheet of blank paper and keep it next to you.

When you are ready, please flip over the first piece of paper with all the numbers written on it. Try to memorize as much of the information as possible. You will be allowed only **5 MINUTES** to complete this exercise, so try to have a timer or a wrist watch nearby. After you have looked at such paper for **5 MINUTES**, (or less if you finish early), then flip such piece of paper back over so that you cannot see it anymore. Give yourself at least two minutes to review the information in your head that you can still remember. Once you are confident that you have reviewed all the information that you have memorized, grab the blank sheet of paper and start to write out all of the numbers in the exact order that you can remember. Also, try to give yourself **only 5 minutes** to write out such information for your answers.

Once you have finished writing out your answers, flip over the original piece of paper with the numbers that were written at the beginning of the exercise. Compare that list with the list of answers that you wrote down based upon your memory, and see how many you got correct. Try to give yourself a grade for such exercise, from 0-100. For every digit that was incorrect, this will count as **2.5 percent**, so you might need to use your math skills or a calculator. See how well you did based upon your knowledge of the Memory Palace, the Dominic Mnemonic, and your previously completed chart of numbers.

In addition, write down the time that it took for you to memorize all of the information, as well as your score for the total number of correct answers. Try doing this once a day for at least a week, and see how well you perform on each task. Here is the list of numbers that I would like for you to memorize. Memorizing numbers is probably one of the first fundamental lessons that I have to teach you, or as Sherlock would say "One must begin at the beginning". By the way, just in case you were wondering if these were just randomly selected numbers, ask yourself if you think that they might be connected in some way to anybody in particular in this book. (hint- think of birthdays and book stories)

01 06 53 05 22 18 59 07 06 19 30 12 02 37 10 04 11 56 81 14

DAY EXERCISE	SCORE (PERCENT/ CORRECT)	TIME (MINUTES, SECOND)
FIRST DAY		
SECOND DAY		
THIRD DAY		
FOURTH DAY		
FIFTH DAY		
SIXTH DAY		
SEVENTH DAY		

AVERAGE SCORE=

AVERAGE TIME=

CHAPTER 4

MEMORY PEGS (LETTERS MEMORY)

Now that we have already learned a lot about memorizing numbers, I think Sherlock would agree that the next lesson to master would be the art of **MEMORIZING LETTERS**. In this chapter, I will be teaching you how to memorize the letters of the English alphabet, since that is what most of us are already familiar with. As you might already recall, there are **26 LETTERS in the English alphabet,** as opposed to only 10 different numerical digits (0-9), which are used today in the English language. And for this lesson, we will try to use all three of the previously mentioned mnemonic techniques that were utilized to memorize numbers. But first, in order to better understand how to memorize letters of the alphabet, it is important to have a better familiarity about the origins of letters themselves. In order *"words"*, let's take a moment to learn a little bit more about the history of the letters of the alphabet.

The history of the alphabet can be traced back all the way to ancient Egypt. Around 2700 BC, Egyptian writing only had a set of 22 figures, or hieroglyphs, which could be used to represent different syllables that each began with a single consonant. Sometimes a vowel could also be supplied by the native speakers to form certain words or phrases. These hieroglyphs were later used as pronunciation guides to help write out grammatical articulations, and then were later used to transcribe actual words and foreign names. Eventually, these 22 figures or hieroglyphs would eventually be categorized into a particular system of sequential ordering and value, called a "script".

The first major phonetic script originated from the Phoenicians. In contrast to two other widely used writing systems at the time, Cuneiform and Egyptian hieroglyphs, this particular script contained about 24 distinct letters. This is two letters less than what we use today in the English alphabet. This system of lettering made it easier for common traders to learn the language and be able to communicate with each other. Another advantage of this Phoenician script was that it could be used to write out different foreign languages, since it only recorded words phonemically, or based on sound.

Later on, this phonetic system was adopted by the ancient Greeks and re-translated several times. In Greece, the script was later modified to add vowels to it, giving rise to the first true alphabet that is still in use today. The Greeks used letters which did not represent sounds that had existed in previous Greek languages. They then later changed these letters to represent the vowels of the alphabet. This marks the first creation of a "true" alphabet, with both vowels and consonants as explicit symbols in a single script. And to this day, it is the most commonly used alphabetical script in the world.

When you think about it, all information that we learn, read, write, speak and hear about, all comes from the usage of the same 26 letters of the alphabet. It is almost incredible to realize that only *26 separate and distinct "symbols"* can be used in so many different possible ways. From words to phrases, to sentences to paragraphs, letters make up pretty much most visual information and knowledge in all aspects of our lives.

And each year, more and more new vocabulary words, phrases, abbreviations and slang, are created so that our English language continues to become a little bit more complex and multifaceted each time. Sometimes, it is a wonder that we are able to keep up with the demands of comprehending and conceptualizing what is written right in front of us. Even at one point, Sherlock Holmes himself was faced with a much more difficult and confusing challenge in quite a similar way.

In one particular Sherlock Holmes story "The Dancing Man", Sherlock Holmes is introduced to a very unfamiliar and mysterious phonetic alphabet system. This particular "alphabet" system was used several times throughout the story, giving clues as to not only the identity of the guilty party, but also the origins of one of the main characters. This alphabet had a simple character *"substitution"* system, where each symbol had two inter-connected forms: a dancing man who is holding a flag to represent the separation of the two words.

In this particular manuscript, the author of such unknown language only used 18 symbols to represent the 18 letters needed in such cypher. Eight particular letters, such as F, J, K, Q, U, W, X, Z, were not used for such purposes. Nor did they have any known related symbols of their own. During the story, Sherlock's new client had received several random sequences of this unknown alphabet at variously different locations throughout the town. From the limited information he already had learned about codes and cyphers, Sherlock was able to use whatever knowledge he had about unknown ancient symbols, in order to be able to decipher and translate the hidden meaning behind this new set of alphabetical clues.

Although most of us would be scratching our heads and wondering how in the world we could ever be able to decipher and decode such an unexpected alphabetical clue such as this, there is one major point that we must remember in order to better understand the psychology behind Holmes's encryption techniques. In this particular story, none of the images that he had observed had any realistic portrayals of any known letters of the English language to begin with. In other words, each symbol would have to be "substituted" for an actual letter of the alphabet.

To the outside observer, such a miscellaneous series of unrelated figures and pictures could easily be misconstrued as either an other-worldly language, or perhaps just a well-planned childish prank. While most people around Holmes would have given up on the idea of being able to understand the meaning behind this hidden message, Holmes decided to take a closer look at the pictures of the "dancing men". He then tried to determine what each figure either looked like or symbolized. In the end, rather than just assume that the "dancing men" figures were just some type of mistake, Holmes realized that, like most other languages in the history of the world, each figure was associated with or "linked" to a particular letter of the alphabet.

Well, now that we have finished covering the topics regarding the history of the English writing system, as well as the story about the infamous Sherlock Holmes mystery "alphabet", let's take a moment and review what the **26 letters of the English language** actually look and sound like. Remember from the previous chapter when we talked about how to memorize the digits of 0-9 by using our eyes and ears? We did this in order to have a better understanding of what numbers really "looked and sounded" like.

Well, now we are going to use the exact system for the letters of the alphabet. Remember, there is not just one particular method that can be used to memorize letters, nor is my particular system the only reliable technique out there. However, I would like to share with you how I learned how to memorize the letters of the alphabet myself. Below is a list of the **26 letters of the alphabet** as well as **two different ways** I have learned to memorize them. (sight and sound, or substitution)

A	looks like a Peg	sounds like "ape"
B	looks like Brass Knuckles	sounds like "bee"
C	looks like a Horseshoe	sounds like "see"
D	looks like a Tongue out	sounds like "deed"
E	looks like a sideways Comb	sounds like "eel"
F	looks like a tooth floss brush	sounds like "aft"
G	looks like an Ear	sounds like "jean"
H	looks like a Step Ladder	sounds like "ache"
I	looks like a Needle	sounds like "eye"
J	Looks like a Cane	sounds like "jay"
K	looks like a Table [tilted]	sounds like "cane"
L	looks like an old weed cutter	sounds like "ail"
M	looks like the form of a spider	sounds like "ahem"
N	looks like Compass [North]	sounds like "end"
O	looks like a Bracelet	sounds like "whole"
P	looks like a Flag on a pole	sounds like "pee"
Q	looks like a Magnifier glass	sounds like "cue"
R	looks like a Ribbon Badge	sounds like "arm"

S	looks like a Snake	sounds like "sis"
T	looks like a Cross	sounds like "tee"
U	looks like a Cup	sounds like "you"
V	looks like Ice-Cream Cone	sounds like "eave"
W	looks like Vampire Teeth	sounds like "uu"
X	looks like a rifling target	sounds like "ex"
Y	looks like a Slingshot | Funnel	sounds like "why"
Z	looks like an Escalator	sounds like "scene"

That seems all rather odd and interesting to say the least. However, just in case you thought that there are only two different ways to memorize letters of the alphabet, let me give you just a little more information that most of us already learned when we were in school. I realize that this is the 21st century, and that most students of education are used to writing down letters of the alphabet on a computer or other electronic devise. However, when I was growing up in school, our teachers used to stress the importance of learning not only the letters of the alphabet, but also how to spell and write them out correctly. That is something that you definitely cannot learn from a keyboard or a printer.

When I was in elementary school, our teachers used to hang a particular graphic design over the top of the chalkboard that stretched from one side of the board to the other. On this long particular artistic diagram, there would be pictures of the letters of the alphabet from A-Z, both in print and in cursive. And underneath each particular letter, was a picture of an object that usually started with the associated letter written above it. Although I don't advocate using only this particular memory system for letters, it was quite helpful as it helped us to remember each individual letter of the alphabet in a more thorough and artistic way.

And just to make learning the alphabet a little more enjoyable as a child, most of our teachers would have us learn the most famous children's song in the history of "elementary" school: ***the alphabet song.*** This was a song that allowed us to actually "sing" the exact order of the letters of the alphabet, rather than just say each letter out loud and possibly forget a few. Once we were able to learn how to sing this particular mnemonic tune, the idea of memorizing the order of the

English alphabet became not only easier, but also a little bit more fun. In a way, this was our first real introduction into the arts of mnemonics.

At this point, I will also give you one more example of how to memorize letters of the alphabet without having to worry about what they actually look or sound like. In this instance, I will follow the same logic and rubric from the lessons that were taught to me while I was in elementary school. For this particular sequence of letters memory, I will give you an earlier and personal mnemonic sequence that was taught to me when I was younger. When I was in school, I was told how to remember each letter of the alphabet based upon the very "first thing" that I could associate with that particular letter of the alphabet. This was similar to the long diagram that was hung over the blackboard, depicting pictures that were alphabetically related to the letters.

In this respect, each letter of the alphabet was connected to a noun that was graphically easy to depict in our minds. For example, the letter A would be associated with a noun that also started with the letter A, such as a person, place or thing. Here is an example of what I learned about the English alphabet when I was in elementary school. But don't worry; you can make up whatever different types of images or figures you would like. You just have to follow the same principles of what I talked about earlier, regarding the "first thing" that you can associate with such letter.

A= apple
B= banana
C= cat
D= dog
E= egg
F= fish
G= goat
H= hat
I= igloo

J= jacket
K= key
L= leaf
M= mouse
N= nest
O= octopus
P= paint
Q= queen
R= rabbit
S= socks
T= turtle
U= umbrella
V= violin
W= wagon
X= x-ray
Y= yarn
Z= zebra

As you can see, each noun can be easily visualized in your mind, without being confused with any other related nouns. Since I have presented you with three different options for memorizing or remembering letters of the alphabet, it is entirely up to you as to which of these three methods you would prefer to use for such purposes. It is up to you if you would like to use any of the previously mentioned techniques such as the Memory Palace or the Link Method. In the previous chapter on memorizing numbers, you were taught that there was a specific code that was designed to be associated with random numbers between 0-9. You were allowed to make up different images or figures for different combinations of such numbers you wanted. Well, in this case, you are free to come up with whatever combinations of letters you wish to use. You can try to combine two letters, three letters, or even four letters if you like. The only thing that matters is that you chose one specific method for memorizing letters of the alphabet, and that you stick with it.

Sometimes you might get lucky, and notice that some combinations of letters remind you of a certain word or phrase. The letters <u>USA</u> always remind me of the American flag. Perhaps you will find combinations of letters that stand for personal things in your life. The letters DSM always remind me of the diagnostic manual that people in the mental health field are very familiar with. Whatever the case may be, you are free to make up whatever system for memorization you want in this instance. Just remember to try to use the same methods of the Memory Palace and the Link Method if needed. All you have to do is place various images along a specific route in one of your memory places, and then go back and rehearse what you memorized, as long as you always remember what each letter "stands" for.

And now, I would like to give you at least two different exercises that you can use in order to better improve your ability to memorize letters of the alphabet. They are both timed and scored exercises that you are free to try at your own convenience. In the first exercise, you will be presented with a total of **20 LETTERS** to memorize in correct order. For this exercise, I will make sure that you don't get the same letters twice. There is a good chance that you will not actually have to memorize every single letter in the alphabet, as there are a total of 26. For the second exercise, I will give you a total of **50 LETTERS** to memorize in correct order. And in this exercise, not only will I be using each and every letter in the alphabet, but I will also be repeating a few of them as well.

In <u>the first exercise</u>, you will need to have at least two pieces of paper. For the first piece of paper, you will need to write down the entire list of letters presented before you in correct order. Make sure you are careful about your spelling, as I will be using all capitals. Next, after you have finished writing down all of the letters, please flip this piece of paper over so that you cannot see them anymore. On the second piece of paper, you will use this as a score sheet. Make sure you have a watch or something to time yourself with. Once you are ready and feel prepared enough with one of your memory palaces, flip the first page back over and begin to memorize the list of letters that you have written. You will be given **3 MINUTES** for this exercise. If you finish early, that is okay, just take your time.

Once you are done memorizing the letters, then flip this page back over so that you cannot see it. Then, give yourself at least two minutes to review in your head what you have just memorized. Once you are finally ready, go over to the second piece of paper and start to write down as many of the letters as you can remember. Make sure that they are all in proper order. Any letter that is not in the proper order will cost you 5 points. Any space left blank will cost you 5 points. Whatever number of correct answers you get, just multiply that number by 5. Record your time on the top of the sheet once you are finished.

For the second exercise, the same rules follow as for the first one. In this instance, you will be given **50 LETTERS to memorize** in perfect order. For this exercise, you will be given **5 MINUTES** to memorize all of the information, as it is going to take you longer than the previous one. And again, make sure that you have one sheet of paper to use as scrap paper, and another to use as an answer sheet. When you are scoring yourself on this exercise, remember that any letter in the wrong order, or any blank space, will cost you 2 points this time.

Please remember to write your times on the top of the paper. I have included the two different lists of letters in the paragraph below, and each is labeled. Don't worry if you don't do well at first, this may take some time and practice. Try to keep track of your scores by practicing the same exercise each day of the week, and record your times. Good luck, and don't forget; when it comes to the concept of individual letters combining to become words, Sherlock would always say that "it's the little things that are infinitely the most important". Also, see if you can find any hidden mystery words located within each line.

EXERCISE 1:

P J W G A X T H C S I E M Y O K Z N U

EXERCISE 2:

QPWIOERUATYMSKDJFHGE

RXNCBLTYOUECWIQKGEFZ

DKSLAVBCNZ

DAY EXERCISE	SCORE (PERCENT/ CORRECT)	TIME (MINUTES, SECOND)
FIRST DAY		
SECOND DAY		
THIRD DAY		
FOURTH DAY		
FIFTH DAY		
SIXTH DAY		
SEVENTH DAY		

AVERAGE SCORE=

AVERAGE TIME=

CHAPTER 5

THE VOCABULARY OF THE VICTORIANS (WORD MEMORY)

For most of us who've grown up in the 21st century, we are all familiar with the specific vernacular and everyday vocabulary words that we tend to use in our daily lives. Most of the time, we don't even stop to think about what we are saying, or if other people know what we are talking about. Simple things such as greetings, questions, answers, commands or invitations, all possess various vocabulary words that most of us are quite used to hearing. Each year, more and more new slang words sneak into our everyday vocabulary as well as our new annual revised dictionaries. And with each new word that comes our way, we begin to realize that the English language has been drastically evolving for many centuries. Unfortunately, it is possible that this particular language will continue to change more and more as time goes on. Boy, I am literally lost for "words".

Sometimes I think about the generational gap that exists between any two people who grew up in different times in this country. I grew up in the 1980's, and we had slang vocabulary words such as "rad", "bodacious", "tubular", "righteous", and "gnarly". Wow, even repeating those words makes me feel old. Whenever I try to use such terminology in the face of a Generation X or New Millennial person, they tend to look at me as though I am crazy or from another planet. This explains why there always seems to be some type of communication problem between people of different generations in this country, as even our own language continues to baffle us. No one really knows how or why new vocabulary words make it into our everyday lives, nor does anyone truly question the validity of such process. However, just because we don't understand the exact same words as each other, does not mean that we can't learn to comprehend what each person's typical usage of speech truly is.

When it comes to the era of Sherlock Holmes, his character grew up in a time in London referred to as the <u>Victorian Era</u>. The Victorian era was a time in European history marked by changes in people's social, political, religious and economic behavior. In the history of the United Kingdom, the **Victorian era** was the period of Queen Victoria's reign, from 1837 until her death in 1901. Ideologically, the Victorian era witnessed resistance to the rationalism that defined the previous period of history. This led to an increasing change towards romanticism and mysticism with regards to religious views, social values, and the arts. It was during this time, that the English language took on a whole new role in the interconnected lives of London's citizens.

Even though I have read many of Sherlock Holmes' stories, which were written from the perspective of his friend John Watson, I could not help but notice that while there were times when I could easily understand the theme and plot of each story, I came across certain vocabulary words that I was not familiar with. This caused me to become confused and to lose focus with the overall plot and theme of the story. Sometimes, I would have to go and look up the definition of such vocabulary word. Other times I would simply guess what the word actually meant, and then moved on. Overall, I realized that, when these stories were written over a century ago, most people unlike me were quite accustomed and used to reading through sentences containing such "Victorian vocabulary".

Just in case you are curious about the meaning of the title "Victorian vocabulary", let me give you a short list of some of the random vocabulary words that I encountered in my *journeys* with the legendary Sherlock Holmes. Rather than give you their individual definitions, I have simply created a list of such words in order to illustrate to you the reasons for my confusion. I also wanted to give you a chance to make up your own minds about whether or not you think you could understand the definitions of such words. Here is a list of some of the words that you might encounter when reading through some of the stories of Sherlock Holmes:

akin, gibe, dubious, effusive, amiss, brougham, astrakhan, obstinacy, august, languid, carte-blanche, inextricable, bijou, mews, ostler, surplice, expostulate, waylay, compunction, outré, teetotaler, panoply, vacuous, dint, penchant.

Many of us are probably sitting at home right now, wondering how we would react to someone else who used such speech in front of us. We might just as likely be standing there, scratching our heads, confused about what the other person was actually saying, as well as trying to figure out how to respond to such exchanges. What is most interesting about these particular vocabulary words is that they were only used in the English language during a certain period of time in European history. After the Victorian Era ended, most of these words began to disappear into the annals of human history, and were inevitably replaced with new vocabulary words to fill in the void. It is amazing to realize the inherent history of the human language.

Words are very important to us all over the world. Without them, most of us would be walking around living like Neanderthals, making grunting noises all day. Words are what make up our whole way of being. From our verbal conversations, to our written language, to our non-verbal communications, we live on a planet where the only way we communicate anything to anyone else is through the use of words. Regardless of whether such vocabulary is still being used today, or is part of an ancient language that nobody uses anymore, words are the one thing that makes us able to truly understand each other more easily. They are the "clay" that builds the "data" that we perceive every day in our respective lives.

In addition to this, one must never forget that in the previous list of vocabulary words from the Victorian era, it should be noted that not all of the words listed were considered nouns. Some of the words were adjectives, and other words were verbs, as well as one or two pronouns. Remember, in the English language, we have a variety of different types of vocabulary words. Things like <u>nouns, pronouns,</u>

adjectives, verbs, adverbs, prepositional phrases, and so on, make up the English language. In most conversations, we don't always use a complete sentence in order to talk to someone else.

It is possible to communicate with others by simply using a few small expressions, or leaving out a few words in each encounter. However, in most literature that is written now of days, readers have hard times comprehending sentences that are written in actual, first hand vernacular. Even though we understand what we might actually say to each other in face to face interactions, it can get somewhat confusing when we try to put down those very same words in print. So remember, what we *say* and what we *read*, are not always the same thing for us.

Now, with that in mind, let's move on to the topic of **VOCABULARY WORD MEMORY**. While vocabulary words are not the same as memorizing numbers and letters, there are still some similarities for both of them. First of all, letters make up words in of themselves. That is not to say that you need to picture each and every letter in a vocabulary word, and then try to memorize the whole thing. If you did that, memorizing a list of vocabulary words would take a very long time to accomplish. Instead, one method that can be easily used to memorize vocabulary words is a method that was previously discussed in past chapters. And that particular method was called the **Substitution Method.**

Earlier back, when we talked about the Substitution Method, we were referring to both letters and numbers. Now we are referring to actual vocabulary words. Well, don't worry; this won't be too much different from the previous lessons. In this instance, what we are going to do is try to "substitute" what the actual vocabulary word looks and sounds like in order to be better able to memorize it. This seems like a simple and basic process, and in a way it is. I will be teaching you a few straightforward methods needed to be able to "transform" one vocabulary word into another one. And once you learn how it is done, you will never again look at vocabulary words in the same way again.

Well then, let's start with some of the Victorian Era words that were previously mentioned in the chapter. The first word that was previously listed was called "akin". Now, just in case you are wondering what the actual word "akin" means, it is defined as "something that is of the same kind as something else". Now this seems pretty simplistic in of itself.

However, if you needed to be able to picture such word in your head, the definition itself does not help out with regards to creating images that can be easy to recall at a later time.

But realize that in this book, you will not have to remember the exact definitions of vocabulary words verbatim. You will only have to be able to remember the actual <u>order</u> of a list of selected words that are listed in a certain way. You have the choice to try to memorize the definitions of whatever vocabulary words you like if you feel like it; however this chapter will teach how to "create images" for vocabulary words so that you are better able to remember the order of such terms.

Going back to the first word "akin", the three most important questions that you must ask yourself are the following; what does the word **look like**, what does the word **sound like**, and what does the word **remind you of**? Everybody has a different way of looking at vocabulary words therefore each person will come up with a different way to break down such a singular word based upon the previous questions. First, from my visual point of view, the word "akin" *looks* like the words "a king", without the letter "g" at the end. In addition, when I *hear* the word "akin", I believe that it sounds like the word "aching" only if you pronounced it with the letters "ch" to look like the letter "k".

And finally, when I think about the word "akin", it makes me think about things that are related to each other, as it reminds me of the phrase "next of kin". Therefore, I have established **THREE** different ways of being able to imagine a word in my head that is neither a noun nor a pronoun. And from there, I can easily come up with random images for the word "akin" and then place those images in a certain location in my memory palace.

Just for example, as the first word in the list is "akin", I will try to picture *a king who is having some aching pain in his legs*. I will then place this image in my memory palace at the first location that I have already set up. And then from there, I will move onto the next word in the list, which is "gibe". Without getting concerned about the actual definition of the word, I already can tell just by looking at the word "gibe" that it looks like the word "glide", and it sounds like the word "jab". Plus, it reminds me of a nautical term that is used to describe a specific rope that is used to tie the sails of a boat (jib). Therefore, for my next image,

I can easily picture *a glider that is getting pulled by a long rope on a boat, which causes it to recoil and jab its owner in the face.*

I know that this is a rather silly and unusual image to think of, but that is the point of using your imagination so that you can visualize such words in your head as they are generally quite difficult to conceptualize. Therefore, for the first two words, I will first imagine the previous example of the king who is in physical pain, and then right next to him, I will picture a flying glider that is being yanked back forcefully by a rope, which causes injury to its rider. This allows me to have created two wild and crazy scenarios or images for my first two vocabulary words.

Also, just in case you were thinking that the only way to memorize vocabulary words was to use the Substitution Method or the Memory Palace technique, I should tell you that there is another method that is just as effective for memorizing vocabulary words. And that method was previously discussed, as it is the **LINK method**. Now, in order to use the LINK method to be able to memorize vocabulary words, the first thing that you would need to do is to take out a piece of paper and put numbers on it. You could number the paper from 01 to whatever number you wanted to end the list with.

So, for this group of words, there are only 25 words listed. In this instance, you could take out a piece of paper and number it from 01-25. And then you would write the actual vocabulary word next to each number. After this is over, you could still use the Substitution Method, by trying to decide what the actual word looks like, sounds like, and reminds you of. Then from there, you would place such an image next to the previous image of the corresponding number listed next to it.

For example, the word "akin" is the first word in the list and therefore it would be placed next to the number 01 on a piece of paper. And from the previous chapter on numbers memory, you already know that the <u>number 01 corresponds to the letters OA</u>. For me, when I think of the number 01, I will automatically picture an <u>image of the letters OA</u>, which for me is an image of a Boy Scout fire. I used to be in the Boy Scouts and joined a secret fraternity known as the Order of the Arrow, or **OA**. Therefore, I chose to picture a large campsite fire surrounded by Boy Scouts. Then after this, I could LINK or attach the creative image of the word "akin", which is the king who is suffering from leg pains, next to such example.

So, if I wanted to memorize the word "akin" as the first word in the list, I would picture my previous image for **01** or OA, and then link that image to that of the king who is in physical pain. In this instance, I will picture a large campfire surrounded by Boy Scouts, while a king is sitting nearby, nursing some aches and pains in his legs. And from there, I have already memorized the first word in the list by "linking" it to the image of the first number of the corresponding numerical order.

Therefore, you now have three different methods that you can use for memorizing vocabulary words in whatever order you want. Please try to practice such methods that were previously listed, and see which one of them seems easier or simpler to use when trying to memorize vocabulary words. The only shortcoming with regards to the LINK method is that you can only use it once for one single list of vocabulary words. The reason for this is because it is difficult to use the number images again in the same day for another list of vocabulary words, without getting yourself confused or distracted by confounding images in your head.

Plus, with respect to the LINK method, I have only showed you how to come up with images for the numbers 00-99, which is only 100 numbers. This means that you can only use the LINK method to memorize up to 100 different vocabulary words at any given time. If you try to use the Memory Palace technique, as long as you have multiple palaces already prepared in your head, you can continue to memorize hundreds and hundreds of vocabulary words, depending on how many memory palaces you have and how many locations you have within them. Still, the decision is yours depending your own personal preference and skill levels.

Now, why don't we try to finally use your new skills for memorizing vocabulary words? For this chapter, I will be focusing on the list of Victorian vocabulary words that was previously listed. You will need at least two sheets of paper for this exercise. On one sheet of paper, you can write out the exact vocabulary words in the exact order that they are listed in this book. You can also choose to put numbers next to each word on the page if you wish to do so. Once you are done listing out all of the vocabulary words on the first sheet of paper, turn such paper over and keep it covered. For your second piece of paper, this will be used as your answer sheet. You can also put numbers on this sheet of paper too if you would like. Once you are ready, take out a watch or a timer, and then flip over the first piece of paper with the vocabulary words written on it. Memorize as much of the information as you can.

For this exercise, you will be given **4 MINUTES TO MEMORIZE** as many words as you possibly can. Once the timer has gone off, stop what you are doing and flip the page over again. After this, take two minutes and rehearse what you remember from the previous list. Then when you feel that you are ready, take out the second page of paper and write down the words in the exact order that you saw them. Since there are 25 vocabulary words, each word is worth 4 points. Remember, spelling counts for each of the words, so if you get even one letter wrong, the word does not count.

Once you are done writing down your answers, grade yourself based upon the number of correct answers you have. If you leave a space blank, or you put a word in the wrong location, please deduct 4 points from your score. If you finish early, record your time on the answer sheet as well. I have enclosed the list of words below in the next paragraph. Practice this a few times over the course of the following week to see how well you get at such an exercise. Here you go; good luck and remember that if you really wanted to learn the definitions for each word, Sherlock would say, "Once you stop learning, you start dying".

akin	mews
gibe	ostler
dubious	surplice
effusive	expostulate
amiss	waylay
brougham	compunction
astrakhan	outré
obstinacy	teetotaler
august	panoply
languid	vacuous
carte blanche	dint
inextricable	penchant
bijou	

DAY EXERCISE	SCORE (PERCENT/ CORRECT)	TIME (MINUTES, SECOND)
FIRST DAY		
SECOND DAY		
THIRD DAY		
FOURTH DAY		
FIFTH DAY		
SIXTH DAY		
SEVENTH DAY		

AVERAGE SCORE=

AVERAGE TIME=

CHAPTER 6

MASTER OF DISGUISES (NAMES AND FACES MEMORY)

Sherlock Holmes had many unique and distinct qualities that made him not only exceptional in his own personal chosen field of work, but also amongst his literary followers throughout the world. Whether it is his penchant for smoking pipes, playing the violin, bare knuckle fighting, or just his love of opera music, Sherlock Holmes was certainly a man of many behaviors. However, one special habit that most people do not always remember about Sherlock was his incredible ability to disguise himself amongst his fellow citizens. Most times, when he needed to create an elaborately fancy façade during his investigations, he would simply locate various pieces of clothing and makeup, and would then alter his appearance in order to look like someone else.

Although Holmes was not a big fan of costume parties, he would purposely disguise himself in whatever manner he chose to. He did this not only to blend in with the rest of society, but also to be able to avoid detection from other criminals. This allowed him to locate valuable pieces of information that most unwary suspects would accidentally reveal to him in many unexpected ways. Sometimes he was able to get a suspect to confess to a crime without the person realizing who they were talking to. Other times, he was able to do reconnaissance in a certain location by studying the social habits of some of the local citizens, without drawing too much attention to himself. Not matter what shape or form he took on during his many adventures across London, Sherlock

Holmes had a "face" that most people did not always recognize until it was already too late.

In this chapter, we are going to be studying how to **MEMORIZE NAMES AND FACES** of people. Now, for this field of memory, we really won't be using too many different codes or ciphers for such purposes. Nor will we be using the Memory Palace Method for such reasons. In this instance, we are going to be relying upon on the <u>Substitution Method</u> along with the <u>Link Method</u>. The reason for this is because most people have names that have letters in them. And from our lesson in the previous chapter about memorizing words, it is usually best to try to use either the Substitution Method or the Link Method in order to better imagine and recall the actual vocabulary words themselves. But before we get too far ahead in regards to memorizing the names of actual people, let's first take some time to review **WHAT A HUMAN FACE TRULY IS**.

First and foremost, let's take a moment to review the exact components that actually make up a human face. Many of us take for granted what a human face really looks like, as we all have similar features on own heads. Eyes, ears, nose, mouth, teeth, jaw, neck, cheeks and eyebrows are just a few of the similarities that we all are born with. Hairlines, skin tone, piercings, baldness, and possible tattoos are features that we can accumulate later in life, depending upon our health and life style. And the best part is that while most of us normally exit our homes in the morning fully clothed and covered up, the one part of the body that always remains naked every day is our face.

We might change our clothes on a regular basis, but we rarely change our face on a regular basis. Therefore, it is highly important to focus on this area of the body. This is because the human face will not only remain similar for years to come, but will also be continuously exposed each and every day. So, in order to better understand what makes a face really look like a face, let's try to examine and delineate the various contours of a human face. Who knows, maybe you might get "lucky" in learning this lesson.

Without getting too much into medical terminology, there are at <u>least *13* different areas</u> of the average human face that can be identified just by looking at them. They are the **hair, forehead, temples, eyebrows,**

eyes, ears, cheeks, nostrils, nose, earlobes, lips, jaw, and chin. The hair is usually located on top of the head. It can be short or long, thin or balding, combed or disheveled, and have multiple different colors added to it. The forehead can have lines, be short or long, and have multiple complexions on it. The temples can have similar features to the forehead as well. Eyebrows can be close or separate, thin or bushy, long or short, large or invisible. Eyes can have multiple different colors, be situated close or far apart, and glasses can also be worn.

Ears can be pointed or flat, large or small, have multiple earrings, and possibly concealed by the hair. Cheeks can be rosy or white, full or flat, colored or pale, and have multiple levels of make-up attached. Nostrils can be large or small, closed or flaring. Noses can be pointed or large, tall or small, red or pale, or have piercings or mustaches near them. And finally, jaws and chins can be strong or weak, round or squared, or covered with facial hair or other piercings. The list goes on and on about the different possible locations on a face that could actively get your attention and make you focus on that one area. By the way, try to figure out why I used the word "lucky" just before describing the contours of the face, this will be alluded to again later in the chapter.

In order to get you better acquainted with the various contours and designs of a human face, one of the best ways to learn how to look at a face is to look at a digital or up-close photographic image of yourself or someone else you know. This can easily be done on social media or by looking at a self-portrait of someone. If you have the chance to acquire such resources, please take a few minutes to actually look at the pictures. Observe each individual section of the face, and take note of what seems **to strike you most as being odd or noticeable about that particular face.**

There is always something special or unique about each person's face. Try to spend some time looking at each section of the face, really take notice about each area and decide for yourself what you think makes each section boring or not boring. This will help you to develop better observation abilities than just trying to stare at another human person's face endlessly in public while they look back at you in terror.

This is the reason why Sherlock Holmes was so effective in fooling so many people when he put on his various disguises throughout his crime fighting career. Whether it was a wig, glasses, makeup, or just some fake facial hair, Holmes always knew how to alter his appearance in order to make it next to impossible for anyone to actually recognize him. Whenever somebody we know has done something different to their face or hair, we immediately take notice of this difference due to the fact that we have grown used to seeing such person in a specific way for a certain period of time.

Granted, if someone we know goes away for a very long time, and then returns with a different type of facial appearance, many of us can simply chalk it up to either aging, life styles, or poor health. However, no matter how much a person's face may have changed over time, somehow we always seem to find one "distinguishing feature" about them that always seem to remain the same throughout the course of our lives.

Now that we have talked about what a human face really is, and why faces always seem to be so special and familiar, the next step to take is to **ACTUALLY *"LOOK"* AT ANOTHER PERSON'S FACE IN REAL LIFE**. Most times, we take it for granted that we have actually taken the time to notice a person's face. Many of us think that this is an involuntary skill that we are all born with. However, whether it is based upon your culture or your social personality, certain people will tend to look at other people's faces in different ways and for different reasons.

While I cannot take the time to explain each and every different manner in which people make face to face contact with each other, I would like to go over one specific method that I have used in my own personal life that has helped me to be more attentive to the various details of other people's faces. In my previous book, I came up with a specific sequence of steps that need to be taken in order to effectively be more prepared in actually noticing what people's faces look like. This particular method that I have come to use is now referred to as the **Lucky 7 Rule**. (hint, hint, **13** and **7**, feeling lucky now?)

Some of the simplest ways to remember a person's name and face can be done in our everyday interactions with people in our daily lives. There are **7 different steps** that can help you to recall people's names and faces better during real life communications. <u>First</u>, look directly at the person while you talk to them, while also trying to minimize or ignore any other distractions around you. Do this for only a few seconds. <u>Second</u>, look for *something* about their face that you either admire or find to be unique. Recall earlier that I told you that there are at least 13 different parts of the human face that most of us can see.

<u>Third</u>, ask the person what their name actually is, and have them tell you the name both slowly and clearly. Try to lean in or put your hand to your ear in order to better hear them. <u>Fourth</u>, repeat the name out loud to them in the course of a short introductory conversation by saying it least *3 times*. Don't repeat their names 3 times in a row too fast as it might look robotic to the other person. Simply use their name in at least 3 different sentences for an initial introduction, such as an initial greeting.

<u>Fifth</u>, just in case the person's name does not sound simple or easy to you, ask the person if they can spell it for you or if they prefer to use a nickname. This will help you to review the information more as you are trying to remember it better. <u>Sixth</u>, try to mention out loud or quietly to yourself whether or not the name reminds you of someone you already know personally or indirectly, such as a family, friend, or celebrity.

<u>Seventh and final</u>, while doing these steps, try to locate the *point* on the person's face that you found to be most noticeable, and then *try to create an image* in your mind that reminds you of the significance of the person's name. Also, just to be safe, when you are done talking with the person, spend a few seconds reviewing the information in your head afterwards. Make sure you got it right, and then ask them if you got their name right by saying "Did you say that your name was ___"?

Now, this does not seem too difficult for most people, as long as you are not surrounded by a group of people all at the same time. This situation would cause you to divide your attention to more than one person at a time, which can be quite difficult. In addition, if you are alone with one person for a few moments, this gives you the chance to get to know the person a little better, even if the conversation is brief and to the point. The main thing that most people don't realize when it comes to memorizing names and faces is not that you really forgot what the person's name was when you first met them. It is that you never actually *<u>heard or even paid attention</u>* to them while they were saying their name in the first place.

By following these 7 steps, you will be forcing yourself to <u>really hear, listen to, and pay attention</u> to what the person is telling you. This will help in being able to recall their names even hours after meeting them. Remember, this usually works best when you are trying to recall people's first names in casual conversations. Plus, just to make it a little bit more fun for you, **7** (<u>lucky number</u>) is the number of steps needed to observe the **13** (<u>unlucky number</u>) features of the human face. Holmes would have enjoyed that special piece of humor as his friend Watson was no stranger to gambling. In addition, 13 was also a very important number regarding the subject of Sherlock Holmes's apartment building. But we will get into that subject in a later chapter for related memory reasons.

As far as the Lucky 7 steps are concerned, the first six steps seems both *elementary* and self-explanatory to most people who are familiar with basic social etiquette. However, the final step seems to be the one step that most people have never heard of or even tried when it comes to memorizing names. **The 7th step** is where you try <u>to come up with or substitute various images</u> of your own to represent each person's name so that it is more meaningful to you. This is where you will have to look at the person's face and try to find something about their face that is special, and then attach an imaginary image to that point on the face while looking at them.

This is important because there is a chance that you will come across a person in your life that has either a first and last name that is completely foreign to you. And you will have no frame of reference available in order to recall it. And no matter how many times you try to rehearse the previous 6 steps in the list, without any images or characters that can be assigned to such person's name, there is little chance that you will ever be able to recall the person's name hours later. This is where we will dive back into an older subject that I briefly introduced to you during our discussion of memorizing vocabulary words. And that subject is called the **substitution method**.

One of the most basic things about trying to remember names for other people is to make the name *meaningful* or *outrageous* in your mind so that you don't forget it later on. In order to do this, it is necessary for you to come up with certain images or symbols in your mind to help you associate a person's name with such an image. The best way to get started in doing this is simply by making up a list of the "most common first names" that you can think of for both men and women. There are so many different last names in this world, that I simply cannot devote an entire book towards them. However, since we don't have the time to go over all of the most common last names in the world right now, let's just try to make up our own list for people's first names.

Be advised, this is just a rudimentary list of common first names for people here in the US. It does not include all the names that most people commonly use on a regular basis, so if I exclude or forget to include anybody's first name on this list, I deeply apologize. So, in order to use the substitution method for names, try to ask yourself **what the name actually looks or sounds like**. Go over and think about each person's name one at a time, and think of the first thing that such name reminds you of (sounds, sights, personal relative).

For instance, the name Irene sounds like an "iron", and the name James sounds like "to aim". So, if I was being introduced to a woman with the name Irene, I would try to locate a specific location on her face and then try to imagine an iron dangling around such area. As well, if I met a man named James, I would try to imagine a bullseye on a specific location of his face as well. Somehow, I think that both of these first names were quite mysterious and frightening in the life of Sherlock Holmes, but I will let you try to figure this one out later. Here are the lists for the most common female and male first names in the US.

COMMON FIRST NAMES FOR WOMEN:

Abby, Abigail, Adele, Alice, Allison, Amy, Angie, Angela, Ann, Anita, Annette, Annie, Annabelle, April, Audrey, Barbara, Beatrice, Becky, Belinda, Bernadette, Beth, Betty, Beverly, Billie, Bobbie, Bonnie, Brenda, Bridget, Britney, Camille, Cameron, Candy, Carla, Carmen, Carol, Celeste, Charlotte, Cheryl, Chloe, Chris, Chrissy, Christy, Christine, Cicely, Cindy, Claudia, Clare, Clara, Clarice, Connie, Crystal, Daphne, Darlene, Debbie, Deborah, Debra, Delia, Denise, Diana, Dina, Donna, Doris, Dorothy, Eileen, Elaine, Eleanor, Elise, Elizabeth, Ellen, Elle, Ellie, Emily, Erica, Eva, Evelyn, Faith, Felicia, Florence, Frances, Gabby, Gabriella, Gayle,

Georgia, Gina, Ginny, Ginger, Glenda, Gloria, Grace, Gwen, Hannah, Harriet, Heather, Heidi, Helen, Holly, Hope, Iris, Irene, Isla, Ivy, Jackie, Jacqueline, Jamie, Jan, Jane, Janice, Jean, Jeanette, Jennifer, Jenny, Jessica, Jessy, Jillian, Joan, Joy, Joyce, Juanita, Judith, Judy, Jules, Julie, Justina, Karen, Kari, Kerry, Kate, Kat, Katherine, Kathy, Kathleen, Katie, Kay, Kim, Kimberly, Kimmy, Kirsten, Kristen, Kristina, Laura, Laurie, Leah, Leslie, Lilly, Lillian, Linda, Lisa, Lois, Louise, Lou-Ann, Loretta, Lorraine, Lori, Lucy, Lucille, Lynn, Madeline, Maggie, Mandy, Marcy, Margaret, Marge, Maria, Marian, Marie, Marilyn, Marlene, Marley, Marsha, Martha, Mary, Mary-Ellen, Melanie, Meg, Megan, Melissa, Meredith, Mirtha, Miriam, Mitzi, Monica, Monique, Myra, Nancy, Natalie, Nicky, Nicole, Nicolette, Nia, Norma, Noreen, Olivia, Olive, Pam, Pamela, Pat, Patrician, Paula, Pauline, Peg, Peggy, Penny, Phoebe, Phyllis, Priscilla, Rachel, Rebecca, Rayne, Renee, Roberta, Robin, Rochelle, Rose, Rosalie, Rosalyn, Roxanne, Ruth, Sally, Samantha, Sandy, Sarah, Sasha, Sherry, Sharon, Sheila, Shirley, Sylvia, Shannon, Shana, Sonia, Sophia, Stacey, Stephanie, Sue, Susan, Sue-Ellen, Susannah, Tamara, Tammy, Teresa, Tess, Tia, Trisha, Trina, Vanessa, Veronica, Vicky, Victoria, Vivian, Wendy, Willow, Winnie, Zelda.

COMMON FIRST NAMES FOR MEN:

Aaron, Abe, Abraham, Adam, Al, Allen, Albert, Alex, Alfred, Alonzo, Alvin, Andrew, Andy, Angelo, Anthony, Archie, Armand, Arnold, Arthur, Austin, Barney, Barry, Baxter, Ben, Benjamin, Bernie, Bernard, Bert, Bill, Billy, Bob, Brad, Bradley, Bradford, Brandon, Brendon, Brian, Bruce, Bud, Byron, Carl, Carlos, Carter, Caesar, Cedric, Chad, Chandler, Charlie, Chet, Chuck, Chester, Chris, Christopher, Clark, Claude, Clayton, Cliff, Clint, Clyde, Cole, Collin, Conrad, Corey, Craig, Curt, Dallas, Danny, Daniel, Darren, Dave, David, Dennis, Den, Derek, Dexter, Dominick, Donald, Doug, Douglas, Drew, Duane, Dusty, Dwight, Earl, Ed, Eddie, Edward, Edgar, Edmund, Eli, Emmanuel, Eric, Ernie, Erwin, Ethan, Evan, Everett, Felix, Fletcher, Floyd, Frank, Francis,

Fred, Frederick, Garrett, Gary, Geoffrey, George, Gerald, Gil, Gilbert, Graham, Grant, Greg, Gus, Hal, Hank, Hans, Harry, Harold, Hector, Henry, Herb, Howard, Hugh, Irving, Isaac, Ivan, Ivy, Jack, Jacob, Jake, James, Jason, Jay, Jerome, Jerry, Jeremy, Jessy, Joey, Joe, John, Jonathan, Johan, Jonah, Jordan, Joshua, Josh, Juan, Julio, Justin, Keith, Kenneth, Kenny, Kevin, Kirk, Kris, Kyle, Larry, Lawrence, Lee, Leonard, Leo, Leon, Leroy, Lou, Louie, Lucas, Lyle, Manny, Mark, Marvin, Mason, Matt, Matthew, Max, Melvin, Morris, Morgan, Nate, Nathan, Nick, Nicolas, Nicky, Noah, Noel, Norman, Otis, Ollie, Owen, Pat, Patrick, Paul, Pauley, Pedro, Peter, Phillip, Phil, Pierre, Preston, Ralph, Randy, Ray, Raymond, Richie, Rich, Rick, Richard, Robert, Robbie, Rob, Rodney, Roger, Rollin, Ronnie, Ronald, Rory, Ross, Russ, Russell, Samuel, Sammy, Scott, Sean, Shawn, Seymour, Steve, Stephen, Stewart, Stewie, Teddy, Terry, Theodore, Tom, Thomas, Timmy, Tim, Toby, Tobias, Todd, Tony, Tristan, Tyrone, Tyler, Victor, Vincent, Vinny, Wayne, Warren, Walter, William, Will, Wilbur, Xavier, Zack

Now, the next most important thing to discuss is how to come up with images for each name that you have listed. Going back to what I said earlier about the **substitution method**, the main procedures used when trying to substitute one word for another, is to ask yourself what does the actual word *either looks or sounds like*. Since we are using names that are associated with people you will possibly meet in real life, I think it would be a good start to try to come up with images for how each individual name <u>sounds like</u>. For instance, when I hear the name "Mary" for a woman, it sounds to me like the words "to marry". Therefore, I instantly think of a wedding dress attached to a part of that person's face. Or if I met a man whose name was John, it sounds to me like the words "to jog ". Therefore, I could picture a series of foot prints going up or across the person's face. I supposed that these types of first names were also quite important in the life of Sherlock Holmes as well.

The final step to take is to be able to look at the person's face, then to find the distinguishing characteristic that grabs your attention (eyes, ears, nose, mouth). And then from there you could try to picture that fictional image <u>doing something to the person's face, as if in a short story</u>. This requires you to start with the focal point on the person's face, and to try to create a small "journey" across that person's face with the imaginary object.

For example, with regards to the woman named Irene, let's say that this person had very red cheeks on their face. I could try to imagine an "iron" is pressing against her red cheeks. This requires a few seconds of trying to look at other locations across the face in order to create this odd imaginative journey about such person. With regards to the gentleman named James, let's say that this person has a receding grey hairline. Well, in this case, I would imagine a "bullseye" pointing at his grey hairline.

That is why I spoke to you earlier about looking at all of the contours of a human face so that you can have a better idea about how to create a small journey along the locations of a human face. In these instances, try to imagine imaginary lines or arrows traveling across the person's face from the focal point to another location on their face where their supposed "name" is supposed to stop. By using such delineative lines or paths on a person's face, you can literally make up a small story occurring on the contours of the person's face, thereby giving you the entire name of the person. This might actually seem to be quite "funny" in certain respects.

However, it is important to remember that you are actually trying to remember something about someone else that is very personal and important to them. While it might be okay to reveal to others what you think about when you try to picture things like cards and numbers, you should try to be very careful about what images you reveal that remind you of various people's names. Sometimes people will either mispronounce my name, or state that my name reminds them of something hysterical. Either way, I tend to feel a little bit hurt by these types of remarks, as my name is very personal to me.

While this might sound simple and innocent to the outside observer, for me I tend to take this very personally. My name belongs to me for the rest of my life and I will hold onto it forever. And believe me; most other people out there are just as sensitive regarding criticisms about their names. So, here is a word of caution for all of you trying to improve your facial memories. **Please, do not reveal to anybody out there anything regarding what images or pictures you have created**

that could remind you of various people's names in the world. This is because you might accidentally offend someone and this will prove costly to you in your social life.

Going back to Sherlock Holmes, one might think that people, who were alive back in his time, might have had different types of facial structures than those of us who are alive today. Well, I can tell you, without having any real expertise in the fields of anthropology that most of our ancient ancestors had facial structures that were somewhat dissimilar to those people that we know in our current lives. However, back in the Victorian Era, most people who were seen up close had very similar facial structures as compared to most people today. Therefore, you don't need to study any information about the history of human faces in order to be able to have a better understanding of facial memory. It is simply based upon your current strength of visual observation, as well as the individual contours of the human face that you are looking at.

When Holmes made it a point to look at another person's face, he did not have to use his magnifying glass or a strong pair of eye glasses, unless he was overlooking the face of a recent murder victim. In the case of Sherlock Holmes, when he looked into the faces of those he interacted with, he would make it a point to examine the whole face from top to bottom. Nobody knows exactly where he would look at a person's face the first time he met them. However, if Holmes ever met you more than once, he would always remember what you looked like from the time before. He would then store such information in his head for recall at a later time.

In some cases, he might ever remember that you have the same shape and tone of eyes as someone else that he has met. Other times he might recall that you have similar markings or imperfections on your face that signify something about your personality. Either way, no matter what you looked like, or how you presented yourself, Sherlock Holmes was guaranteed to take notice of something about your face that either intrigued him or got his attention. In effect, he made it his mission to actively "study" each and every person's face he met, as if he was reading a book that he found to be interesting.

Now, since I cannot actually quiz you specifically on memorizing people's names and faces, I will ask you the reader to complete some basic homework assignments so that you can be better prepared for the future challenge of facial memory. In this instance, what I would like for you to do is to make up a list of the **100 MOST COMMON FIRST NAMES FOR BOTH MEN AND WOMEN.** You do not have to use the list that I already provided you, unless you would prefer to do so. After you have come up with at least 100 different first names for both men and women, list them on a sheet of paper, either numbered from 1-100, alphabetical or from top to bottom.

Then, I would like for you to use the <u>Substitution Method,</u> and write down a word or a phrase next to each individual person's name that reminds you of that particular name. This will be the associated "image" that you can try to remember for each face. You can decide if you want to look at what the person's name looks like, sounds like, or what the name reminds you of. Feel free to mix it up however you would like to. There will be some names that are very familiar to you for your own personal reasons, and then there will be other names that are funny sounding to you as well. Just use your best inner instincts for each name if possible.

Once you have created your master face list, try to cover up one side of such list. You can cover up the side that has the actual names written on it, or the side that has the associated word or image listed on it. Remember, you don't have to make this perfect, just try to come up with an image for each person's name that you can easily see in your mind. Try to quiz yourself to see if you can remember what each name is associated with, or vice versa. You might even be able to draw some pictures along with such exercise if you want to. But for now, just try to get familiar with all of the names on your list as well as the associated images that are linked to each name. Keep covering up one side of the paper each time and try to see if you can easily memorize the names and their associated images if possible.

Finally, once you feel that you have a good grasp regarding all of the common first names and their associated images, try to use these techniques out in the real world. This will not be needed if the people that you run into are people that you are already familiar with. Only use this technique around people that you have never met before in your life. Try to use the <u>Lucky 7 skills</u> that were listed earlier, along with your memory of the person's name and the associated image for such.

Give yourself the opportunity to really *test your facial reading abilities* by really looking at the face of the person that is talking to you, without trying to stare them down or make them feel uncomfortable. Once you continue to practice this technique over and over again, you will soon discover that it will get easier and easier for you. Pretty soon, you will be able to walk into a room full of strangers, and be able to remember the names and faces of many people before the end of the night.

Here is *one assignment* that I liked to give myself when I first started using this particular memory technique. Each time I would go out to a new convention in my life, whether it be a party, wedding, or some other type of formal event, I would try to memorize at least <u>10 DIFFERENT PEOPLE'S NAMES AND FACES</u> before I would leave such an outing. At the end of the night, I would then try to make it a point to go over to the 10 people that I had already spoken to, and confirm with them what their names truly were. I would tell these people that I had remembered their names, and would proceed to call out their names to see if I was correct. Each time I did this, people would take notice of me for taking the time to memorize their names so perfectly. They would automatically treat me differently the next time they would see me.

Sometimes you will be around dozens and dozens of people all in the same night. Don't feel that you have to be able to memorize all of their names and faces, unless you get the chance to actually see and speak to each and every person at such occasion. However, if you would like to try to improve your ability to remember people's names and faces better, first start out small and continue to work your way up.

At first, start off by memorizing the names and faces of at least **10 people** that you don't already know at some large social occasion. Then the next time, try to increase that number to either **15-20 people**, depending on the size of the audience. Once you have shown that you can memorize the names of faces of at least **30 people** all at once in a single evening, you will prove to others as well as to yourself, that you have mastered the technique of facial memory. So go ahead and try your *luck* out, and if you end up seeing someone that you have already met before, don't forget the immortal words of John Watson as he stated "Oh how I've missed you, Holmes."

CHAPTER 7

"YOU HAVE BEEN IN AFGHANISTAN" (PERSONAL INFORMATION MEMORY)

For those of you out there who have never read any of the stories about the legendary detective Sherlock Holmes, there is always one story that I often enjoyed reading when it came to the subject of PERSONAL INFORMATION. Before I go on, when I say "personal information", what I am referring to is not just intimate knowledge about an individual's personal life, but also other relevant factors such as social demographics. In this chapter, we will be focusing on how to memorize personal information about other people and how to recall such information at a later date and time.

In one of the very first stories about Sherlock Holmes, entitled "A Study in Scarlet", Sherlock Holmes gets the chance to meet his future roommate, and partner in crime detection, Dr. John Watson. In their first encounter, Sherlock is busy working in a laboratory, overlooking some type of scientific experiment. During such time, a friend introduces him to John Watson, who is looking for a potential roommate as well as a place to stay. During this introduction, Sherlock looks over at Watson for several seconds and then approaches him. Instead of asking him how his day was or if he would like to have a seat, Sherlock stares right at Watson and states "you have been in Afghanistan, correct?"

Watson is astonished by such revelation, as he had never revealed such personal information to Sherlock before. He then asks Sherlock how he could have known such information about him, to which the brilliant detective explains that he had noticed several different things about his clothing, his behavioral mannerisms, his voice, as well as his physical condition. Talk about a major moment of deductive brilliance.

Although this book will be focusing on the field of memory improvement, we will not be delving into the study of non-verbal behavioral cues. This would take too long and is not something that can be taught simply by reading one book. However, in this encounter, Sherlock is able to deduce several personal things about Watson during their first interaction. He is able to figure out that Watson has recently returned from active duty in Afghanistan, as well as the fact that he is suffering from an injury he sustained in combat. In addition, Sherlock is also able to realize that Watson is an army doctor, that he has some family relationship issues, and that he is struggling financially due to housing problems. And throughout the rest of this story, as well as the rest of their future journeys together, Sherlock never truly forgets any of this *personal information* concerning his favorite companion, John Watson.

Sometimes, it is easy for some of us to be able to deduce certain personality traits or behavioral characteristics of people that we meet in public. Whether it be the tone of their voice, their clothing styles, or their physical appearance, certain pieces of information seem quite easy to notice and recall, once we have rehearsed such information over and over. However, you don't actually need to repeat the personal information of someone that you have just met in order to be able to memorize it. There are other ways to be able to memorize personal information about others. This is based upon some of the lessons that were previously mentioned in some of the earlier chapters, such as the Journey Method, the Link Method, and the Substitution Method.

Before we get too far ahead, let's first take a moment and talk about what is the difference between demographics and personal information. **Demographics**, without getting too clinical in definition, is information that is concerned about various factors, such as race, ethnicity, age, gender, socio-economic status, nationality, ethnicity, and religion. These are generalized terms that are often used to categorize different aspects of a person's life. Some variables cannot be changed as they might be based upon a person's birthright; others can be changed based upon circumstantial conditions. Either way, demographics are usually constant variables about a person's life that make up part of their individual personality as well as their psychological disposition.

However, personal information does not always have to be about a person's demographics, although it can be overlapped from time to time. **Personal information** can be more specific and detailed related facts about an individual, which are usually a lot harder to decipher simply by just looking at them, as in the case of the initial meeting between Sherlock and Watson. It would not be difficult for Sherlock to ascertain that Watson was a Caucasian male who was visibly injured, as this type of information could be easily ascertained simply just by looking at him. However, the ability to determine other information about him, such as his profession, his military experiences, his family complications, as well as his financial struggles, would be far more difficult to deduct just from a single glance. And yet, such information about Watson would be considered to be his *personal information*, which is what we are going to be focusing on in the next paragraph.

In this chapter, we are going to focus on how to remember an **individual's personal information** and how to recall such information when necessary. Unfortunately, there will be a lot more images and codes that need to be used in order to remember such information. The good news is that *you get to decide* what codes or images you want to use, as most personal information cannot be classified the same way as names and numbers. In order to help you realize how far you have come in your journey of memory, I am going to review some of the things that you already know from our previous discussions about memory. Then I will give you more choices about what other types of personal information you can easily recall, and how to do it.

Before we start to talk about the process of memorizing personal information, I think it might be a good idea to first talk about how to actually store or record a person's personal information in order to better memorize it. In order to do this, let me first tell you a historical story. During the 1940's, the current president of the United States at that time was a man from my home state of New York, famously known as

Franklin Delano Roosevelt. Very few people ever knew that this great and powerful man, whom the country looked up to for so many reasons, was secretly unable to even stand up or walk on his own two legs. Yet, most rhetorical historians would agree that, when it comes to the *person* occupying the office of presidency, *image* itself is more important than *actions*.

A lot of prominent individuals who were alive during that time have mentioned that if they had owned a television set in their households during the 1903's, it would have been unlikely that this country, which was already recovering from a Great Depression and World War II, would have ever chosen to elect a man who was sitting in a wheelchair. However, there was one individual behind the scenes who was working on FDR's inner staff. And this one person seemed to know a lot more about how to influence the general public as far as making the voters see past FDR's physical handicaps, and instead focus their attention on his political character.

That gentleman's name was **James Farley,** and he was a legend among the political kingpins of his time. He was probably one of the greatest politician campaign managers of the twentieth century. However, in the memory world, he was also a legend for being able to recall the personal information of the most powerful and rich benefactors that FDR had met in the course of his presidency. And he did this by creating a system that is still widely used to this day, called a **Farley file**. In such a file, he would include a photograph of the face of the person that FDR was supposed to meet, as well as some personal data about each individual that he could commit to memory. And by remembering the names and personal data of the most important people that FDR was counting on to get re-elected, this small town, farm working high school dropout, was able to get FDR the political money and the electoral votes that he needed to help him get re-elected more than once.

Just in case you were wondering what an actual Farley File looks like**, there is not one specific template or example that can be shown**. However, in my own personal life, I have created my own version of a Farley File for when I am preparing to meet a new client for the first time. Usually, when I have a new client coming to me, I almost always get a hospital discharge report about them, which includes a lot of personal information in specific formats. Yet, I don't always feel as though I really need to memorize all of the information that is printed about each person. Instead, I have devised a Farley File that looks something like this:

NAME
BIRTHDATE
ADDRESS
FAMILY RELATIONS
HOSPITALIZATIONS
MEDICATIONS
DIAGNOSIS
SYMPTOMS

For most people out there who are not familiar with the field of mental health, this particular list seems odd and unusual. And if I were not familiar with mental health, I too would agree. However, in this instance, what I have done is instead of focusing on every single detail about a new client, I chose to focus on the *most relevant information* that is needed to be known about the person at the moment that I first meet them.

That is not to say that I don't care about any other relevant information that pertains to their lives. It is just that, when I first meet a client that is coming out of the hospital, these previously listed items are the things that are most relevant towards completing their initial paperwork, as well as to be able to get a better understanding of why this individual has come to my office in the first place. In other words, I am simply focusing on the most pertinent information that I need to know in order to further continue to do my job effectively for such person. And from there, I try to "file" such information away in my head for future references.

Throughout most of the stories written about Sherlock Holmes, he demonstrates to his colleague Dr. Watson, as well as to several other police officers, that he likes to keep a specific type of personnel "file" on most of the previous criminals that he has already arrested. He also likes to keep such information regarding the personal life of certain influential people living around London at the time. Although in his day, there were no computer systems or metallic filing cabinets that could be used for such purposes. Instead, he used to write down a lot of the personal information about all of the major criminal suspects that he met from his previous cases. Then he would keep such information in a large dresser draw where he would have such materials labeled in alphabetical order.

Each piece of paper would include information about the person's name, job title, address, past crimes, financial worth, as well as their family relationships. And each time Holmes would have some free time to himself, he would always make it a point to go over all of this random information, one piece of paper at a time. That way he could always refresh his memory about the personal characteristics of many of his past enemies. This would allow him to be able to remember such information at the right moment during the course of a criminal investigation, just in case he ran into someone else related to another criminal at the time. It seems like each criminal that he had arrested in the course of his career, already knew that their days were in fact "numbered", based upon this organizational system.

For now, let's get off the topic of Sherlock Holmes and talk about what you already know about personal information. And then from there, we can move onto what you are about to learn in the future. If you remember from one of the earlier chapters regarding how to memorize numbers, I asked you to come up with <u>100 different characters or images</u> for all numbers between **00-99**. As you may recall, each number is related to a different set of letters or initials that stand for the name of a character associated with each number. There are several bits of personal information about a person that can easily be recalled just by using numbers. Here is your first lesson on how to memorize a person's *<u>birthdate, Social Security number and telephone number</u>*, simply by using this system. Certain pieces of personal information such as birthdays, Social Security and phone numbers can only be delineated by using a random series of numbers. Therefore, this next lesson will be quite self-explanatory, or in the case of Sherlock, "elementary".

When it comes to talking about a person's birthday, most of us are familiar with expressing it in the following order; <u>xx-xx-xxx</u>. However, in order to remember a person's birthday, one thing that you should try to do first, is come up with an image which stands for the term "birth". I have two images in my mind that I can use interchangeably at any given time. I chose to either picture a baby in a thick blanket, or a birthday party hat on top of a cake. Either one reminds me of the day that a person was born. You can come up with whatever images you would like for your own personal use. And for those of you who are familiar with a yearly calendar, you should probably already know the following order of the 12 months of the year: January (**01**), February (**02**), March (**03**), April (**04**), May (**05**), June (**06**), July (**07**), August (**08**), September (**09**), October (**10**), November (**11**), and December (**12**).

Previously, we talked about how to LINK different pieces of information together, one right next to each other. You would do this so that they form a long string of information that can easily be remembered once you decode the images in your head. For remembering a birthday, you could try to lead off by first picturing whatever image you can think of regarding the concept of "birth", as the first image in your head. This will always allow you to remember that the following string of numbers is related to a person's birthday, and not some other piece of personal information. So, the first image you should think of is the image that you can create for the concept of "birth". Then the next image that you could create is whatever you chose to construct for any one of the 12 listed months of the year. This will be the second piece of information in the standard depiction of a person's birthday.

In order to picture the month of the person's birthday, you would first start out by coming up with your own image for what a birthday represents, and then move onto the right side of that image. It is there that you could attach the character for the corresponding month of the year. After that, the next piece of information would be the day of the month for such birthday. And you could attach another image for that number to the right side of the image of the month of birth. Then do the same thing for the year of birth. It is up to you if you want to use 4 digits for the year or just two numbers.

So, for example, if you have a friend whose birthday is January 6th, you could write it out as 01-06, followed by the year. In this instance, the image I have created for 01 is a Boy Scout, and the image I have created for 06 is Oskar Schindler. Therefore, if I wanted to remember that my friend's birthday was January 6th, I could picture an image of a large birthday cake that has a Boy Scout standing to the right of it, while he is giving a piece of cake over to Oskar Schindler. And from there, I can easily recall that my friend's birthday is January 6th. By the way, just in case you were not aware, *January 6th* is Sherlock Holmes's birthday!

Also, if you are interested in trying to remember certain days of the week, remember that there are only seven days in a week. There are different methods that you can use in order to recall such days when it comes to remembering birthdays. For instance, you could try to sound out each day of the week, and try to come up with a "substitute" word for each image. I like to think of Sunday as a big, large sun, glowing down on me. Monday is characterized by lots of money in my mouth, as this is usually when I cash my pay check. Tuesdays is usually pictured as the Tooth Fairy wearing a tutu dress, hence the words repeat.

So, if the birthday was May 22nd and the day of the week was Sunday, you could imagine the image for Sunday first, and then the characters for 05 and 22 to the right of such initial image. For this instance, I would first imagine a large sun (**Sunday**) beaming down on Owen the Elephant (**05**) (cartoon character I created as a child) while he is standing next to Bruce Banner, also known as the Hulk. (**22**). I am simply using the PAO method again, as each image is connected and dependent upon each other. And from there, you have a set of images to remind you of the day of the week for a person's birthday, as well as the actual birthdate itself. I bet that Arthur Conan Doyle would have appreciated that particular storyline.

In addition, if you were also wondering about how to remember certain times of the day, there is another good method that I am familiar with. My late grandfather was active in the Marine Corps, and as a child he used to quiz me about how to read the time of the day in military time. For example, 3pm would be considered 15:00 hours, or fifteen hundred hours. This means that you would count the hours from midnight going forward simply by adding the numbers as the hours continued on. 3am is 03:00, or 03 hundred hours, and 3pm would occur 12 hours later. Therefore, if you wanted to picture what 3pm looks like in terms of using your mnemonic images, you could easily picture your images for the numbers 15 (AE) and 00 (OO)with a <u>large clock</u> next to it. This lets you know what time of the day it is if you are interested in including that into your personal data section.

    <u>Phone numbers and Social Security numbers</u> are just as easy to do, as you can come up with another image for a **phone** and another image for **Social Security**. And then attach a series of pictures to the right side of either of these images in order to create a chain. For a telephone number, I can easily picture an old telephone ringing loudly. For Social Security, I can easily picture an old person with checks in their hands. And once that image is locked in, I just go about implanting any of my images to the right side of such introductory image. Remember, phone numbers are usually 7 digits long, unless you need to remember the area code, whereby it then become 10 digits. Social Security numbers are only 9 digits, so try to be careful about how you organize your codes or images, as you don't want to recall too much information that is not needed.

    Also, it would be beneficial to try to use your various memory palaces in a certain order so as to be able to store such information in different rooms or loci. Just be sure to remember to include the images associated with birthdays, Social Security and telephones as the <u>introductory</u> images for each room. And then if possible, try to start off in your memory palace by recalling the person's first and last name by using word associations.

    So, if I were to try to remember my aunt's birthday and phone number, I could easily picture her first and last name as two different images in the first room of my memory palace. Then this would be followed by images representing her birthday and day of the week in a second room. And then other images representing her phone number would be placed in a third room, and so on. Now, I have some type of organizational tools needed in order to recall such information about an important person in my life. These are the things that you already "know" about from previous lessons.

    Now, let's start to focus on the information that you <u>don't already know</u> (sound familiar?). As you realize, there are endless categories of personal information that apply to any given person. Some of it can be ascertained simply by talking to such person, others items you would have to look up through some type of *investigative* methods. And all of this data can easily be stored in the other rooms or locations in any of your memory palaces. But for now, the following topics of personal information are going to be discussed: **addresses, nationalities and ethnicities, vocational jobs, cars, family relations, hobbies, favorite foods, and educational degrees.** By being able to do this type of memory challenge, as well as using the previous lessons regarding names and numbers memory, you will now be able to effectively recall at least **12 different pieces of personal information** just for one individual person.

With regards to **addresses**, it is quite easy to recall the actual number of the residential household or the zip code of the town that a person lives in. You would simply use your previously 100-character codes for numbers. However, when it comes to remembering the actual street and state for such addresses, here are some suggestions that you can use in order to help recall such residential information more accurately. First, I will present to you a list of the **50 states of the United States of America.** Although Sherlock Holmes lived in London, we will instead be focusing on the country of the United States. As you remember from your past chapter on word memory, I would ask for you to come up with an associated image or character for each of the 50 states listed below so that you can easily recall such image later.

As far as how I have done, I usually try to think of what the name of the state actually *sounds* like or *something very iconic* about the state itself. I am from New York, so I can easily picture a Big Apple or the Twin Towers. As for maybe Hawaii, I can picture a volcano or a hula girl. Other states might require some more thought and imagination. For now, just try to think of an image that either *sounds like, looks like, or is historically associated* with each state, and write that information next to each name of the states listed below.

Alabama	**Montana**
Alaska	**Nebraska**
Arizona	**Nevada**
Arkansas	**New Hampshire**
California	**New Jersey**

Colorado	New Mexico
Connecticut	New York
Delaware	North Carolina
Florida	North Dakota
Georgia	Ohio
Hawaii	Oklahoma
Idaho	Oregon
Illinois	Pennsylvania
Indiana	Rhode Island
Iowa	South Carolina
Kansas	South Dakota
Kentucky	Tennessee
Louisiana	Texas
Maine	Utah
Maryland	Vermont
Massachusetts	Virginia
Michigan	Washington
Minnesota	West Virginia
Mississippi	Wisconsin
Missouri	Wyoming

As far as how to recall the <u>actual name of any city, town or village,</u> simply use the same <u>substitute word system</u> as before with the US states. Just ask yourself what the name of the location actually *sounds or looks like*, or if you know something personal about such district. You would then attach that image to the left side of the image for any of the states, and then just add the zip code to the end of it. As far as the actual <u>street address</u> is concerned, continue to use the same substitute word system as before. However, if you would like to create your own mnemonic images for the **actual types of US roadway designations** that are currently in use, I have included a list of such names for future reference. Chose whatever images come to mind when you hear or see any of these following words. I have included several images that I personally use for each type of travel route.

TYPE OF ROADWAY	ASSOCIATED IMAGE
Alley	Alley cat
Avenue	Van with new sign in window
Boulevard	Large bull in a yard
Bi-Way	Ocean waves crashing
Causeway	Santa Clause on moving sleigh
Court	Legal court room
Drive	Automatic car stick shift
Highway	Toll booths
Interstate	Large battery
Lane	Yellow lines on road
Road	Concrete blocks
Route	Compass on GPS machines
Street	Stripes on a rainbow
Park	Swing set
Terrace	Terrorist cell
Way	Arms waving

Let's try to visualize an example of a person's actual address, including their residential house number, city and state. One particular address that I truly like to use as an example is the Office of the President of the United States. The White House address is **1600 Pennsylvania Avenue in Washington DC 20500**. So, if I wanted to remember not only his face, but also his actual work address, I would picture the name and face of the president in the first room of my memory palace. Then I could picture the numbers (16) and (00), which stand as the letters AS and OO. Accordingly, in my system, these characters are represented as Arnold Schwarzenegger (AS) and James Bond (OO).

For example, in the next room of my memory palace, I could picture Arnold drinking from a martini glass while shooting a gun from a concealed pocket, just like James Bond. This would give me the numbers 1600. And then on his right side, I could imagine the image that I have for the state of Pennsylvania, which is a pencil sharpener with lots of pencils coming out of it. And then next to this image on the right hand side, would be another character that would represent the word <u>Avenue.</u> For me, "avenue" is a van with a sign posted in its front window. So, next to that image I could picture a large pencil sharpener with lots of pencils, drilling themselves into the front sign of an old van into a street.

Then in the next room or possibly the following location, I could imagine a character for the city of <u>Washington</u>, which is simply just an image of a washing machine with lots of clothes coming out. Next to the right of that figure are the letters <u>DC</u>, and such letters will always pertain to the associated character for the number <u>43</u>, which is usually Dick Clark. So, I will imagine a washing machine loaded with lots of clothes, while Dick Clark is standing next to it, trying to pull a largely lit New Year's Eve ball from inside of it.

Finally, when it comes to the zip code, I can easily picture the images for the following numbers, <u>20 and 50</u>, or (BO) and (EO). The letters BO represent for me, our former president Barack Obama, and the letter EO represent comic actor Ed O'Neill. Therefore, standing to the right side of Dick Clark, would be an image of Barack Obama (20) putting women's shoes on his own feet (50), while standing near a large hole (0). And there you have it, the **entire address** for the White House, in just several different associated images. All of the information is linked from left to right, in different rooms or different locations within each room of one of your memory palaces. Talk about having "national" pride, right?

With regards **to nationalities or ethnicities**, I have always found that people attach deep personal pride and respect to their nationalities simply because this characteristic will be with them for the rest of their lives. Now, I do not exactly know how many different nationalities there are in the world, but I have attached a list of the <u>50 most common nationalities</u> that I have seen currently in the United States. If I have excluded or forgotten to include your own personal nationality, I apologize as I cannot come up with images for every single nationality. Feel free to come up with any images for any nationality that you feel comfortable with, based upon what the nationality actually sounds like, looks like, or simply reminds you of.

So, if I wanted to think about an image for the nationality of Italian,

I could picture an image of the Leaning Tower of Pisa, with a large pizza smothered on top of it. And if I wanted to remember that one of my relatives was Italian, I could picture the name and face of one of my relatives standing alongside this creative image for the nationality of Italian. If you don't want to create images or try to remember a person's nationality for personal reasons, then that is entirely up to you.

Also, try not to share with people how you came up with such images for nationalities or ethnicities, as you don't want to insult such person by telling them that their nationality reminds you of an obscure scene. This is similar to the lesson from name memory in regards to avoiding hurting other people's feelings. So for now, here is the list of the **50 most common nationalities in the US**.

Afghan	**Indian**
Amish	**Iraqi**
Arab	**Irish**
Austrian	**Israeli**
Australian	**Italian**
Belgian	**Jamaican**
Bosnian	**Japanese**
Brazilian	**Jerusalem**
Cambodian	**Korean**
Chinese	**Louisiana Creole**
Colombian	**Mexican**
Cuban	**Native American**
Czech	**Norwegian**
Danish	**Pakistani**
Dominican Republic	**Polish**
Dutch	**Puerto Rican**
Egyptian	**Portuguese**
English	**Russian**
Finnish	**Scottish**
French	**Somali**
German	**Spanish**

Greek	Swedish
Haitian	Turkish
Hispanic	Venezuelan
Hungarian	Vietnamese

Interestingly, one of the most common and popular questions that I get asked by other people, who are trying to get to know me, is the question of **what I do for a living**. I always enjoy being asked that question from others. But what if the person who is talking to me has absolutely no idea what my actual job really means? In this new day and age, there are so many different types of job titles, positions, and designations out there that most of us just simply shake our heads when we hear what other people do for a living. Sometimes it does not matter what the other person does for a living. We are just thankful that such person has a job in the first place.

However, if you don't understand what field of employment a person generally has, here is another list of the **25 most common fields of vocational employment** in the US. Even though you might not be able to recall exactly what a person does for a living, you can make them feel better just by remembering what field or "specialty" they practice in. So for me, my field of work is listed in the section labeled Community and Social Services. And for that, I could easily picture a person handing out bread to the homeless at a food shelter. Again, feel free to come up with any related images or characters that you can think for each field of practice. Most of the jobs mentioned are so common nowadays that we might already know someone else who is employed within such field.

Architecture and Engineering
Arts, Design, Entertainment, Sports, and Media
Building and Grounds Cleaning and Maintenance
Business and Financial Operations
Community and Social Services
Computers and Mathematical sciences
Construction and Extraction

Education, Training, and Library
Farming, Fishing, and Forestry
Food/drink Preparation and Serving Related
Healthcare/medical Practitioners and Technical
Healthcare Support staff
Installation, Maintenance, and Repair
Legal, correctional, law enforcement
Military or Armed Services
Life, Physical, and Social Science
Management, entrepreneur, or administration
Office and Administrative Support
Personal Care and Home Service
Production of products
Private Business store owner
Protective Services
Private practice employment
Sales and Related products
Transportation and Material Moving

For many people, owning a car is like owning a new part of oneself. Sometimes the car defines you, other times it tends to categorize you. That is why when I meet a person who is driving a nice new automobile, one of the first things that I like to ask them is what is the make and model of the car. I do not know much about cars, but sometimes just acknowledging what a person drives is a compliment in of itself. Sherlock Holmes grew up in a time when there were no actual vehicles to be familiar with. Therefore, I have attached a list of the <u>36 most common brands of vehicles </u>that have been made in the US in the past decade. If I have left any out, I apologize as I am only going by my own personal experiences, and don't always know if other people out there have ever owned any newer and more advanced vehicles. Here is a list of the **<u>36 most common brands of vehicles</u>** if you would like to create any images for such.

Acura	Kia
Aston Martin	Lamborghini
Audi	Land Rover
Bentley	Lexus
BMW	Lincoln
Buick	Maserati
Cadillac	Mazda
Chevrolet	Mercedes
Chrysler	Mini
Dodge	Porsche
Ferrari	Ram
Fiat	Rolls Royce
Ford	Saab
Honda	Subaru
Hyundai	Suzuki
Infiniti	Toyota
Jaguar	Volkswagen
Jeep	Volvo

When I was younger, I used to look at my **own family tree** and wonder how each person was related to another. There was no major key or legend that was used to delineate each relationship to each other. In mental health, it is a common practice to create what is known as a family **genograph**, which is a picture of the client's name in the center of the page, followed by a bunch of other names with various symbols around such name. Each symbol defines the types of relationships between all listed persons. However, in the real world, that is not always possible as most of us don't walk around with a sheet of paper when we talk to others. Therefore, if you have the lucky chance to get to look at another person's family tree or just want to get a general idea of the family composition at an upcoming gathering, here is a list of the **30 most common relationship statuses** that exist among most people in the US. Try to think of a concrete image that you can associate with each <u>relationship status</u> and get ready to be able to know an entire family tree by "heart".

Father
Mother
Brother
Sister
Stepmother
Stepfather
Stepbrother
Stepsister
Grandfather
Grandmother
Great-grandparent
Aunt
Uncle
Cousin
Niece
Nephew
Daughter
Son
Grandchild
Friend
In Law
Neighbor
Colleague
Boss
Wife
Husband
Fiancée
Girlfriend
Boyfriend
Ex-spouse

In addition to the 30 most common relationship statuses, there are also 6 most common marital statuses that can also be included in this list. Such marital statuses can easily be associated with most of the 30 most common relationship statuses listed above. However, this will only apply to people who are old enough to have been married in the first place. It wouldn't make any sense to associate any of these statuses with a child of such sorts. Try to think of an image for each type of status listed below and then attach that image to the name of the person who you are trying to memorize if you "like". Therefore, **the 6 most common marital statuses** are:

SINGLE
MARRIED
DIVORCED
WIDOWED
ENGAGED
SEPARATED

Perhaps the easiest question to ask a person in a causal conversation is about what likes or dislikes the other person has. This will usually lead to a long and verbose conversation if the person is comfortable in talking to you. When it comes **to hobbies, recreational activities, and favorite foods**, this is usually the easier topic to memorize. You only have to picture the activity or food item itself, or something related to either one. If you have never heard of the particular activity or food item, simply ask the other person to clarify it for you or ask how it is spelled. This will help you to be able to visualize it in your head and place it in another room of your memory palace. So if the person likes playing the violin or smoking tobacco, simply just imagine someone actually doing any of these activities in another room of your memory palace. If the person likes eating pasta or pizza, simply picture such food items in another room of your memory palace in the same way.

As far as **educational degrees** are concerned, don't worry about trying to recall the exact field of study of the person involved is, or the exact words for their educational degree. I have a master's degree in social work; however just remembering that I have a master's degree in the field of mental health is good enough. The only thing that we are going to be covering in this section is what <u>exact level of education</u> the person truly has, not what subject they have studied. As far as knowing what areas of study the person has worked on, or what institution they graduated from, there are literally thousands and thousands of schools throughout the US as well as hundreds of different academic related fields of study.

When it comes to receiving education in the US, there are only a few degrees that can be received from institutions of higher learning; <u>high school, community college, bachelor level college, graduate school, or doctoral school.</u> In this case, the letter **M** would relate to someone with a *master's* degree and **D** would relate to someone with a doctorate or PhD if you want to use that term. You probably already have an image for the letter D as it can be represented by the number 04. Remember earlier when you were coming up with images for <u>your 100 number characters or persons?</u> Well, it looks like some of these letters can be used to correlate with those numbers that just happen to appear on the list below. So, if you think about it, if you were someone who has a high school (HS) degree, that would translate to the number 86, which is my character of Han Solo. If you have an associate's degree in the science of any related subject, then that would be the letters AS or 16, which is my image for Arnold Schwarzenegger.

Also, if the person did not finish high school, simply ask them <u>what grade level</u> they last finished, and just remember the actual <u>number</u> for that grade, such as 11th grade or 12th grade. Below are the following types of educational degrees that can be earned from going to school in the US. And if you can combine this imagery with the information regarding **what field of work or vocation** the other person is involved in, then you can easily ask somebody a question that sounds like "I know that you have a <u>master's</u> degree in the field of <u>social services</u>, am I correct?" You could remember this information by placing the name and face of such person in one of your memory palace rooms, followed closely next to the images for the actual subject of *social services*, and then the image for the letter *M*.

Grades 1-12= associated letters (OA, OB, OC, OD, etc)	
GED= General Educational Degree (74)	
HS-	High School graduate (86)
AS-	Associates in the science of (16)
AA-	Associates in the arts of (11)
BS-	Bachelors in the science of (26)
BA-	Bachelors in the arts of (21)
MA-	Masters in the arts of (M 01)
MS-	Masters in the science of (M 06)
DA-	Doctorate in the arts of (41)
DS-	Doctorate in the science of (46)

Well, by now I think you are probably wondering when you will ever have the chance to be able to use such a memory technique in the future. Perhaps you might try to memorize personal information at your next reunion with friends. Maybe you will try to use this technique the next time you go to work and speak with your colleagues and constituents. You might even try to ask a total stranger some questions about themselves using the same rubric, though I would be careful about doing such a thing. However in this case, I have prepared a little exercise for you to complete in order to see how well you can memorize personal information about a person, and then recite it back in perfect order.

In the table listed below, I have included biographical information about <u>4 real life people</u> who have passed away many years ago. I will not use their last names out of respect to any and all remaining loved ones or family members they might have. So for now, you will only be presented with their first names and last initials. However, despite my attempts at trying to remain discreet, I will state that most of their biographical information is actually completely true. I have organized such materials into the field of a chart. Each row is labeled based upon the specific piece of personal information attached to each person.

For this exercise, I am going to ask you to take out two pieces of paper. On one sheet of paper, you are to write out all of the information that is presented below in the exact order and structure that it is presented in. This may take a few minutes as each person will have at least <u>10</u>

pieces of personal information listed for each one of them, for a grand total of 40 pieces of personal information. Once you are done writing down all of the information as it appears in the book, please turn this piece of paper over so that you cannot see the answers. You will be using the second piece of paper as your answer sheet. Try to draw a blank chart on the second piece of paper with the same number of rows and columns as was presented to you. You can also label each row if you chose to.

Before you get started on this next assignment, take out a timer or a stopwatch and prepare to time yourself for this exercise. You will be given **only 6 minutes** for the memorization part of this exercise. Take a few minutes and review one or two of your memory palaces, and then go over some of your mnemonic codes for personal information. Once you feel that you are ready to begin, flip over the previous piece of paper where you wrote down all of the information that was previously listed. Try to memorize as much of this information as you can.

After six minutes is over, turn this piece of paper back over again so that you cannot see it. If you finished earlier, this is also okay, just as long as you jot down your allotted time. Take a few minutes to go over the information in your head before you move on. Once you feel confident in your memory abilities, go ahead and grab the second piece of paper and start to write down as much of the information as you can remember. Fill in the appropriate spots with the appropriate personal information. Remember, spelling and sequential order do count.

You will be given at **least 6 minutes** for recall in order to write out your answers, as sometimes it takes longer to write such responses down. Since there are 40 pieces of personal information to remember, you can give yourself **2.5 points for each correct answer**. Blank spaces do not count, and incorrect spelling and disordered information is also considered wrong. At first, this will not be an easy exercise to complete, so don't be too upset if you don't get a perfect score. It may take a few attempts to get used to such a mnemonic exercise. So, I advise you to try to repeat the same memory exercise again another day in the week under the same circumstances. That way you will have enough time to be able to forget the information so as to be able to try to remember it again later. See how well you do the second, third, or even fourth time you try. Just remember to follow the same rules and procedures that were previously listed.

So, for now, here is the personal information about the *4 select individuals* that I would like for you to memorize. Now, you are probably wondering why I chose to pick these particular individuals. Well, the reason for this is because each one of them has something very important in common with each other. **THEY ALL ARE THE REAL LIFE INDIVIDUALS AND FIGURES THAT WERE THE INSPIRATIONS FOR THE CHARACTER KNOWN AS SHERLOCK HOLMES.** Good luck, and I will see you in a "flash".

NAME	Joseph B	Henry L.	Jerome C.	Walter P.
BIRTHDATE	12/02/1837	05/08/1836	03/11/1844	01/26/1862
NATIONALITY	Scottish	Scottish	English	English
VOCATION	Surgeon	Govt Official	Police Officer	Illustrator
EDUCATION	Doctorate	Masters	High school	Bachelors
STREET ADDRESS	2 Melville Court	24 Royal Circus Rd	10 Moss Center	10 Bromsgrove St
SPOUSE'S NAME	Edith Katherine	Isabella Jane	Amelia	Edith
CHILD'S NAME	Benjamin	Henry Jr.	Charles	Leslie
FAVORITE HOBBY	Forensics	Social parties	Costumes	Play Actor
FAVORITE FOOD	Tea/crackers	Steak and chops	Oatmeal	Fish

DAY EXERCISE	SCORE (PERCENT/ CORRECT)	TIME (MINUTES, SECOND)
FIRST DAY		
SECOND DAY		
THIRD DAY		
FOURTH DAY		
FIFTH DAY		
SIXTH DAY		
SEVENTH DAY		

AVERAGE SCORE=

AVERAGE TIME=

CHAPTER 8

FLASH TECHNIQUE (CLOTHING MEMORY)

For many people growing up in the 21st century, clothing has taken on a whole new meaning. It seems as though with each new generation in this country, a whole new line of clothing becomes part of our daily lives. Whether it be items that you wear on your legs, arms, shoulders or your head, no matter how much we try to stay ahead of the trend, there always seems to be some new type of clothing style coming out that we are just getting used to. I guess that is why we call it a "fashion trend" as it seems to be like a movement headed in a certain direction.

What is most difficult for many of us is the reality that most of the clothing we used to wear back when we were younger, is now considered archaic or ancient, compared to today's standards. Although the clothing styles that we used to wear can still fit us the same way they did years ago, we often take the risk of walking outside and being noticed by other people in very strange and confusing ways. It is quite difficult to be able to predict how clothing styles are going to change and why they are going to change. This is unless of course you work in the fashion industry or are a highly respective expert in the field of costume designs. For most of us out there in the real world, the only way to know what is "in" and what is "out" is to check and see what is currently available in our monthly shopping catalogs.

Sherlock Holmes was not a fashionable individual by any standards. He was not concerned with looking his best on most days whether he was inside or outside the office. However, he also did not want to present himself as looking like a pauper or a poor person to others around him. Instead, he would often wear the same kinds of garments whenever he would go out on a case with his loyal companion. According to most of his biographies, he was well known for wearing a tweed suit or frock-coat, along with his signature deerstalker hat. In addition, he would also choose to wear a long grey travelling-cloak and close-fitting cloth cap. However, whenever he was alone going over his notes from a previous case in private, he would often sit in the corner of his cluttered office and would be wearing a mouse-colored dressing-gown, or sometimes a purple colored one.

During the 1880s, in Victorian era London, formal evening dress for men consisted of a dark tail coat with trousers, a dark waistcoat, along with a white bow tie, and a shirt with a winged collar. During such time, the dinner jacket or tuxedo, was used in more relaxed formal occasions. Tweed or woolen breeches were used for rugged outdoor pursuits such as shooting and hunting. Knee-length topcoats, and calf-length overcoats, were often worn in winter. Men's shoes had higher heels and a narrow toe for each foot. Hats were crucial to a respectable appearance for both men and women. To go bareheaded was simply not proper. The top hat was the standard formal wear for upper- and middle-class men.

For women, the styles of hats changed over time and were designed to match their outfits. The women's shoes of the early Victorian period were narrow and heelless, either in black or white satin. During the 1850s and 1860s, these shoes were slightly broader with a low heel and made of leather or cloth. From the 1870s to the twentieth century, heels grew higher and toes more pointed. Low-cut pumps were worn for the evening. Also, around that time, clothing could be made more quickly and cheaply through the use of fabric stores. Advancement in printing and production of fashion magazines allowed the common people to participate in the evolving trends of high fashion, opening the market of mass consumption and advertising.

Despite Sherlock's lack of fashionable presentation or sophistication, he often was very familiar with the typical styles of clothing that was expected of certain individuals in London during that time. He would spend unusually long periods of time outside his apartment, noticing the various clothing styles of the people that walked past his residence. He would often take notice of certain articles of clothing that often got his attention. Sometimes he noticed that there was something wrong or different about what other person were wearing. In one classic story, he is able to observe that his colleague, Dr. John Watson, had scratch marks on his shoes which were ultimately caused by a maid trying to forcefully clean the dirt off of such items. He realizes that ordinarily, if Watson had not left his apartment to come out to see him, his shoes would ultimately have remained clean.

Whether its 19th century London, or 21st century America, people's clothing usually tells a lot about the personality of the person who is wearing it. Although I will not be getting into how to analyze a person based upon their clothing, I will be going over how to take notice of the differences in how people present the attire that they are wearing. There is <u>no real scientific method</u> that can be used in order to analyze a person's personality simply based upon their choice of clothing. Sometimes people will try to experiment with trying on new things in order to see how well they enjoy such changes. Oftentimes, when a person tends to wear the same types of clothing day after day, it eventually becomes apparent that there is some element of their personality that can be drawn by noticing the patterns in their clothing choices. Yet, from just a single viewing of a person walking down the street, it would be impossible to really know anything personal about such person simply by just looking at their outer wear.

One of the most common questions that people are asked when they are trying on some new article of clothing is whether or not such clothing actually fits. For some reason, nobody ever asks the other person whether or not such clothing matches. A lot of times, the only thing that most people are generally concerned about, is if the clothing feels comfortable on their bodies, especially when they are changing into such outfits. When they come out the changing room and look at themselves in a mirror, the next question that they ask themselves is if the clothing looks good on them. This is a question that most of us have been instructed never to ask out loud to another person that has just come out of the dressing room. However, when we as the consumer look at ourselves in the mirror, we generally try to imagine ourselves walking outside wearing such outfit, and wondering how we are going to be perceived by others.

Clothing can be worn in many different ways. Sometimes it fits loosely as well as tightly. Clothing can be displayed in a mismatched color fashion, or in a highly organized color fashion. Sometimes, our clothes can be exhibited in a wrinkled and disgusting manner. Other times our clothes can look neat and pressed to the outside observer. Occasionally, there might be holes or stains in our outfits, other times the colors might actually fade away due to frequent washing. No matter what you chose to buy in the store, it is never actually observed by the public until you chose to wear it outside on your own terms.

In addition, there any many different companies and agencies out there that are responsible for making new lines of clothing every day. Whether it is small shops that you might see in the local shopping mall, or designer stores that you might find in high end sections of major cities, there are always new names coming out with new articles of clothing. Sometimes this can be happening so fast, that it seems impossible to be able to keep up with such "trends". Speaking for myself, I can tell you that I am not in any way an expert on clothing in this day and age. I could not tell the difference between Dolce-Gabbana, Gucci, or even Michael Kors. I would not know the dissimilarity between a V neck and a halter top if I tried to study it. Either way, while there are certainly some people out there who are considered fashion experts or even garment "geniuses", I for one AM NOT.

However, even though I cannot understand the difference between a stiletto heel and a hiking boot, I have discovered a new method that can be used to be able to actually **MEMORIZE ARTICLES OF CLOTHING**. I know that this must sound kind of silly, considering my lack of knowledge on the subject. However, while I do admit that I am not familiar with many different styles or companies that are out there on the market, I am confident that I know that there are only several locations on the human body where clothing can actually be worn. This allows me to be able to focus my attention on various spots of the person's body and try to remember which article of clothing is covering it. Instead of being concerned about knowing the differences between different styles of clothing, I will only be focusing on how to remember <u>WHERE</u> specific articles of clothing are worn on a person.

When I first started watching movies and television shows about Sherlock Holmes, I was mesmerized by his abilities to not only remember certain amounts of information about other people, but to be able to do so both quickly and effortlessly. There was one scene in a BBC television series about Sherlock Holmes, entitled "The Hounds of Baskerville", where Sherlock Holmes and Watson are sitting in a pub by a fire place. During such time, Sherlock is visibly shaken by an earlier experience with an otherworldly canine villain. While he is drinking alcohol in the hopes of calming himself down, his companion tries to ask him some questions in the hopes of getting more information from him about their current case. However, Sherlock is so startled by what he has seen that he cannot seem to make sense of it. It is during this time that Sherlock begins to have doubts about the one part of his body that he cherishes more than anything; his brain

At one point, Sherlock gets so angry and upset with the situation that he chooses to prove to Watson that he is still in control of his amazing deductive skills by analyzing the clothing styles of a couple sitting right next to them. He is able to accurately determine the relationship between the two people at the table, as well as their respective jobs, personal habits, and current medical ailments. Although Sherlock is not entirely familiar with every single style of clothing available on the market, he is able to take very special notice of each and every garment that both parties were wearing at the time. And what is more impressive, is that Sherlock was able to look such persons up and down and to be able to tell something about them in a "*flash*".

Now, there is a reason why I chose to use the word **FLASH** when talking about the speed at which Sherlock seems to be able to notice things about other people's clothing. The word itself "flash" is how I chose to remember **WHAT AREAS OF THE HUMAN BODY** to pay attention to when I am looking at a person who is standing in front of me. When I used to work at the prison, I was told by some of the officers about how to visually scan what an inmate was wearing and why it was important to do so. For most of the officers I worked with, they would often try to observe the inmates from a distance as opposed to being up close. And when they used to observe inmates from a distance, they would often look at the prisoner, not from top to bottom, but actually from bottom to top. And this got me thinking about how to come up with an acronym that could be used to better remember what places on the human body to take notice of. In order to better explain my "*flash*" method, please take a moment and observe the following diagram:

HEAD	
SHOULDER	SHOULDER
ARM	ARM
LEG	LEG
FEET	FEET

In order to observe a person from bottom to top, the first area to focus on is the person's **FEET**. The word "feet" begins with the letter F. So, the first thing I try to pay attention to is what type of footwear the individual is wearing. Now like I said, I do not know about different types of clothing, however I can tell the different between a hiking boot and a sandal. So, before I take notice of anything else, I will chose to look at what type and color footwear an individual is actually wearing. Things like sandals, boots, crocs, work shoes, sneakers, flip flops, high heels, or even just bear feet, are just some of the different footwear to expect to see on a person when they are standing in front of you.

Going back on one of his earlier stories, there is a scene where Holmes takes notice of what type of shoes his companion Dr. John Watson is wearing after he has arrived to the office late on a rainy day. During their brief conversation, Holmes is drawn to pay attention to the scratch marks on Watson's shoes as he is standing next to Holmes while they are drying off near the fireplace. In that instant, Holmes points out that Watson has several scratch marks on his shoes. He is wearing a certain formal type of shoe wear, as this was the custom for a British doctor during that time in English history. And after only a few seconds, he is able to deduce that Watson's servant girl was responsible for causing some scratch marks as she was probably trying to clean off such shoes in a careless and haphazard manner. Naturally, Watson is astounded by Holmes brilliant deduction, and realizes that this is the first location that Holmes was looking at, as Watson had previously been out in the rain and had already gotten his shoes wet as a result. This gives a whole new meaning to the phrase "the game is AFOOT."

The important thing to remember is to be able to have an actual image in your head for what the particular foot item sounds like or looks like to you. When I picture a flip flop, I can instantly think of a large bunny walking carelessly. When I think of crocs, I often picture a crocodile as it sounds just like the word. And from this image, I then place it in my <u>FIRST LOCATION</u> of my memory palace, as this is the first item that I will be paying attention to. Either way, the most important thing to do is to come up with a list of different types of footwear that people are well known to wear in this current day and age. I have attached a list of **8 DIFFERENT TYPES OF FOOTWEAR** that are normally seen by most people, as well as some associated images that I have used before. If you know of any other types of footwear that were not included on this list, please add to it at any given time.

<u>NAME OF FOOTWEAR</u>	<u>ASSOCIATED IMAGE</u>
Work shoes	**Buffering brush**
Sneakers	Person running
Flip flops	Floppy eared bunny
High heels	High ladder
Boots	Cowboy on a horse
Sandals	Beach and ocean waves
Crocs	Crocodile
Socks	Christmas stockings

Let's go back to the previous example from the British BBC TV series, regarding the infamous scene in the pub, from "The Hounds of Baskerville". This is where Sherlock and Watson are talking in front of the fireplace, and Sherlock is deducing the personal information of the couple sitting behind him at the table. In this scene, he is able to pay attention to the other woman's pants, and begins to notice that she has some dog hairs on her pant legs. From this information, Sherlock already knows what possible type of dog she must own, and how big this type of pet might be. In this situation, he did not get his deduction correct from looking at her shoes, but instead was able to figure out this information by looking at her pants.

When traveling up the person's body, the next area to pay attention to is the person's **LEGS**. The word "legs" starts with the letter **L**. In this instance, you would next want to focus on what types of leggings or pants the individual is actually wearing. Things like blue jeans, trousers, shorts, sweatpants, skirts, or even just a large belt, are all various items that are usually found around or near a person's leg area. When I was a child growing up with my family, I usually had a lot of fun when it came to thinking about people's different pants styles. There were lots of different advertisements back then, so certain images of random clothing are easier for me to remember than others.

When I think about blue jeans, I usually try to imagine that legendary poster of Bruce Springsteen. If I think about shorts, I can also picture an image of Daisy Dukes. And for either image, I place that image in the SECOND LOCATION of my memory palace, as it is the second item to remember. For this reason, it is important to come up with a list of different articles of clothing to expect to see on a person's legs or thigh area. I have included a list of **10 DIFFERENT ARTICLES OF LEGGING CLOTHING** that are usually found on people in this current time, as well as some images that I have chosen to use for such purposes. If you have any other information about any different types of pants or leggings that are available out there, please feel free to update the list as needed.

NAME OF LEG COVERINGS	ASSOCIATED IMAGES
Work pants	Iron pressing against wrinkles
Blue jeans	Bruce Springsteen image
Skirt	Scottish kilt
Khakis	Hacky sack

Shorts	Daisy Dukes
Trousers	Farmer overalls
Sweatpants	Runner on treadmill
Dress	Wedding dress
Winter pants	Snowman
Belt	Cowboy belt buckle

In one of the most recent major blockbuster movies, regarding the character of Sherlock Holmes, there is a scene where his friend John Watson meets Sherlock Holmes at an expensive restaurant for dinner. During this engagement, he is able to introduce Holmes to his new fiancée, Mary. After they have exchanged glances with each other, Mary asks Sherlock if he would be able to deduct information about her just from looking at her. Holmes then looks at her hands and notices that there is a small mark on her ring finger where she used to be wearing a wedding band. From this quick observation, he is able to deduce that Mary had a former fiancée whom she is no longer with. Although she is not happy with his rude behavior and lack of moral social skills, he is nevertheless correct in his deduction simply by just looking at her hands and arms.

The next items to pay attention to are what articles of clothing are covering the persons' **ARMS**. The word "arms" starts with the letter **A.** In this situation, you would want to pay attention to whatever items are located on an individual's hands, fingers, wrists, and forearm area. Often, if the person is wearing a long sleeve outfit, then it is hard to see what is on their wrists and forearm area. In this case, you could just focus on the overall article of clothing that they are wearing. However, if the person is wearing short sleeves, then there are many different items that they could have on their person. Also, from my own personal experience, most people who have tattoos on their flesh often have them in the arm area of the body. They might also have tattoos on their legs and other locations on their bodies; however this seems to be the most prominent location to find such body art.

With regards to the arm areas of the body, I tend to have pre-conceived images for random items that can be found in such locations. When I was growing up as a child, I used to have relatives in my family that used to wear lots of rings on their fingers, even on both hands. I also am a child of the 1980's, and one of my favorite candies was a specific ring shaped lollipop, called the Push Pop. It was a large lollipop that could be worn on the person's finger temporarily. Whenever I think of an image for a person's rings, I tend to picture a Push Pop, as this is an easy image to conjure up. And then I put such image in the <u>THIRD LOCATION</u> of my memory palace, as it is the third item to pay attention to. Below I have created a list of the **8 DIFFERENT ARTICLES OF ARM CLOTHING** that can be typically found on the arms area of the human body, in addition to some images that I like to use for such reasons. If you have any ideas about any other types of garment wear that can be found in such area of the body, please feel free to create an image for such item and expand upon this list if desired.

NAME OF ARMS COVERING	ASSOCIATED IMAGES
Rings	Push Pop
Watch	Pocket Watch
Bracelet	Arm brace
Wristband	Resistance band
Gloves	Baseball glove
Long sleeves	Sails on a boat
Tattoos	Tattoo needle and gun
Press on fingernails	Large claws

In the same feature film regarding the character of Sherlock Holmes, there is another scene where he is chasing after his on-again, off-again girlfriend Irene Adler, after she has come to pay him a visit. In this scene, he is hoping to get more information from her as she has just made him a generous offer for a new case to take on. However she will not say who she is working for. After a few minutes of secretly chasing after her, and putting on some improvisational disguises, Holmes is able to bump into her horse-drawn carriage and notices that she is sitting next to a grown man, who has some chalk stains on his sleeve and shoulder. From this quick glance of the total stranger, Holmes is able to deduce that the person she is sitting next to is probably a well-educated college professor. This is based upon the fact that most college professors at the time used to write their lectures on their chalk boards. Sometime such person would get their shirts dirty with such chalk. And he simply came to that conclusion just by noticing what type of shirt clothing the man was wearing.

And of course, the next item to focus on with regards to the human body would obviously be the **SHOULDERS**. The word "shoulders" starts with the letter **S**. In this respect, what you are trying to focus on is whatever item of clothing is covering the persons' shoulder area and chest area. This is usually one of the easiest forms of clothing to pay attention to. Most of us are very much aware of whatever shirts we are wearing as this is often the first place people tend to pay attention to when they see us. However, not all articles of clothing are the same for such a location. As I stated before, I do not have much expertise in the field of fashion, nor do I expect to achieve such a desired state. Despite my lack of knowledge in such field, I have noticed that there are several different items of clothing that are usually found on the person's shoulders and chest area.

When I was younger, I used to think that everybody in my school used to wear T-shirts to class each day. Most of them did, however a few chose to be creative and wear different outfits. I also used to like playing both golf and baseball when I was younger, as these were sports that I tended to gravitate towards. So when I think of a t-shirt, I tend to imagine either a tee ball being hit into a shirt, or a shirt with golf tees tacked into it. Then I place this item in the <u>FOURTH LOCATION</u> in my memory palace, as it is the next item to pay attention to. Below I have created a list of **10 DIFFERENT ARTICLES OF SHOULDER CLOTHING** that are usually seen by other people in the community, as well as some associated images that I like to use when I am trying to remember such. If you feel that there are any more items that can be added to this list based upon your own personal knowledge, please feel free to update the list as needed. Then place whatever images you prefer to use for such purposes next to it.

NAME OF SHOULDER RELATED CLOTHING	ASSOCIATED IMAGES
T-shirt	Tee ball hitting shirt
Tank top	War tank
Button down shirt	Sewing and button kit
Blouse	Blowing a house over
Sweat shirt	Shirt covered in sweat
Sweater	Old rocking chair
Fleece	Flock of geese
Suit jacket	GQ picture of suit
Coat	Large fur minx
Flannel	Handyman

In one of his later stories, entitled "The Golden Pince Nez", Sherlock Holmes is called upon to investigate an unsolved murder. During such time, the case is further complicated by the fact that there are no major "eye" witnesses or physical clues left for him to determine who the guilty party is. There is a scene where Holmes is investigating a crime scene and comes across a pair of golden colored eye glasses, known as pince nez. Although he is not sure who the actual owner of the glasses is, Holmes is able to deduce that the person who was wearing them is probably a female with certain facial features and has a fondness for wearing formal clothing. Although most people in the room are baffled by such outrageous claims, he is nevertheless correct in his deduction about the real individual who is actually the owner of the glasses. It is from this instance that Holmes is able to make accurate assessments about another person, simply by focusing on what is located on their head.

And finally, the last area to focus on when trying to size up a person in a "flash" is the **HEAD** area. The word "head" starts with the letter **H**. In this area, you will focusing on whatever garment items are located on the person's head, face, or neck area. This is usually also one of the easiest areas to remember, as we always tend to look at people's faces when we are talking to them. The longer we are looking at a person, the more we will tend to pay attention to this particular area of their body. Plus, we already devoted an entire chapter into how to remember people's names and faces. There were many different areas of the face and head that were covered. So, this will be the most familiar of all of the areas to go over when it comes to clothing memory.

I used to wear thick glasses when I was younger due to poor eye sight. This led me to get made fun of a lot in my younger days of playing in the playground. However, despite my negative experiences with near sightedness, I remember that I always used to enjoy playing music during my teenage years, as I was very good at entertaining other people. So, when I think about a person wearing a pair of glasses, I often picture a very large pair of glasses, similar to the ones worn by legendary singer Buddy Holly. This helps me to associate such image with this particular piece of facial jewelry. Then I place this item into the <u>FIFTH LOCATION</u> in my memory palace, as it is the last item to remember. Below I have created a list of the **10 MOST COMMON ARTICLES FOR THE FACIAL AREA**, which are typically seen each day in the real world, as well some images that I have made up. You are free to add any new articles that I have not already thought of as well as some images to attach to such items.

<u>NAME OF FACIAL OR HEAD WEAR</u>	ASSOCIATED IMAGES
Scrunchy	Pony jumping through a hoop
Earrings	Large circular rings chiming
Hat	Lincoln-style hat
Necklace	Mr. T gold necklaces
Glasses	Buddy Holly large glasses
Hair clips or braids	Weaving machines/ getting braided
Piercings	Hell-raiser face
Scarf	Snowman with scarf wrapped
Sunglasses	Top Gun fighter pilot
Facial hair	Face of a Yeti

Lastly, there is one more lesson that I have forgotten to teach you that might be even more effective in enhancing your ability to remember people's clothing. Whether you like it or not, people's clothing always tends to have certain **COLORS** that make them more special. Regardless of whatever type of shoe wear, pants, shirts, or head wear you chose to display in the real world, it will always have a certain color, or arrangement of colors added to it. The good old days of wearing clothing that always seemed to match is all but over. Most people will chose to wear a variety of colors in their outer garments, no matter what combinations they present themselves in. And for that reason, I will be teaching you a quick lesson on how to remember **CERTAIN COLORS**.

First of all, I just want to let you know that I am not an artist, nor have I ever been one. With regards to my lack of knowledge regarding clothing, I have even a lesser knowledge about all of the various colors that make up this world. No matter how good my eyes are, I could not tell you the difference between magenta and velvet. However, I am not attempting to make you an artist in any way. Unless of course you have some experience in such area, then in that case you are already familiar with such lessons. For this lesson, we will be going over **13 DIFFERENT COLORS** that are generally found on various items in the world, as well as some images that I have chosen to create for such reasons.

For this lesson, you will have to remember the previous lesson regarding the <u>LINK Method</u>, as you will be linking the image for the actual color to the image of the article of clothing. For example, if I told you that I liked to wear a blue T-shirt, you would have to remember an image for the color "blue" having some type of interaction with the image for a t-shirt. But before we get too carried away, below is a list of the **13 most common colors** that I have seen before in my life. If you have any other colors that you are already familiar with, please attach them to such list as well as an image to help remember such color for future reference.

VISIBLE COLOR	ASSOCIATED IMAGE
Red	Bouquet of roses
Blue	Ocean waves
Green	Shamrocks and grass
Yellow	Bananas
Orange	Orange juice
Pink	Pepto drink
Black	Oil drill
Brown	Large coffee mug
Grey	Space craft
Purple	Wine bottle
White	Clouds
Tan	Tanning booth
Gold	Gold chest

Going back on the previous example of a blue T-shirt, in this instance, you would have to attach an image for the color "blue" having some type of interaction with the image for a t-shirt that is associated with it. So for example, if I wanted to imagine a person wearing a blue T-shirt, I would try to imagine the image for the color blue (large ocean waves) followed by an image for a t shirt (tee ball hitting a shirt). Remembering the LINK method that was explained before, and by using some of my associated images, you could try to imagine a large ocean wave crashing down on a tee-ball as it is hitting a shirt. And from there, you would have a linked image of a person wearing a blue t-shirt, which you would place in one of your locations in your memory palace.

Now, for your final challenge, I will be presenting you with <u>FIVE FICTIONAL PEOPLE</u>, who are wearing 5 variously different articles of clothing per person. This makes for a grand total of **25 different**

articles of clothing or outer wear. The names of such people will not be discussed at this time. I will have the information about their clothing displayed in the form of a chart. Before you start such exercise, go over your related images for each article of clothing listed, as well as all of the mentioned colors. Also, go through one or two of your favorite memory palaces for such lesson. You will need two sheets of paper for this particular exercise.

On one sheet, you will need to copy down all of the listed information exactly as it is presented to you. Take as long as you need to write down such information. On the second piece of paper, please create a chart similar to the one that you previously saw on the first piece of paper, except leave this one BLANK. After you have written down all of the necessary information, flip this page over so that you cannot see it again. Then when you are ready, flip this page back over. You will be allowed **FIVE MINUTES** to memorize as much of the information as you possibly can.

Once your time is finished, flip over the first piece of paper so that you cannot see the answers. After that, go ahead and grab the second piece of paper with the blank chart on it. Take a minute or two to review such information in your head. At this point, give yourself **SIX MINUTES** to write down as much of the information that you remember about each person. Remember, if you put the wrong piece of information in the wrong location for any one person, it counts as a mistake. Blank spots will also count as zero points. Since we have **25 different articles** of outerwear, each correct answer will be worth 4 POINTS.

If you finish early, please record your final time. This might be a difficult exercise to complete as you are probably not familiar with memorizing clothing. That is okay, put the exercise away and try it again the next day, and possibly the day after that. Give yourself time to forget all of the information and then see how much better you do the next time around. By the end of the week, you will see a drastic improvement in your scores. Good luck, and as Sherlock would say "The game is afoot, into your clothes and come".

PERSON 1	PERSON 2	PERSON 3	PERSON 4	PERSON 5
Red sandals	Black work shoes	White sneakers	Green boots	Barefoot
Blue jeans	Grey pants	Orange shorts	Purple trousers	Gold sweatpants
Gold rings	Silver watch	Red Tattoos	Pink gloves	Pink wristband
White blouse	Tan button down	Tan sweater	Yellow tank top	Brown coat
Black Sunglasses	Yellow earrings	Blue hat	Grey piercings	White scarf

DAY EXERCISE	SCORE (PERCENT/ CORRECT)	TIME (MINUTES, SECOND)
FIRST DAY		
SECOND DAY		
THIRD DAY		
FOURTH DAY		
FIFTH DAY		
SIXTH DAY		
SEVENTH DAY		

AVERAGE SCORE=

AVERAGE TIME=

CHAPTER 9

"SENSE" SATIONAL LITERATURE (CURRENT EVENTS MEMORY)

Before the arrival of the Internet and digital computers, most people across the globe could only count on getting information about the daily news from their local newspapers. Each morning, people around the world would wake up and walk outside to their front steps, where they could find a rolled up copy of the current day's newspaper. Inside such everyday editorial, one would most likely find lots of information on a barrage of topics, such as foods, weather, comics, and local advertisements. However, there was always one section of the newspaper that most people could always count on to provide them with the most up to date information on any particular subject in the world. And that special section of the newspaper is something we refer to as "**current events**".

Current events are generally considered to be reportable information about significant happenings that have occurred throughout a particular region on a specific day. Events such as sports, local gatherings, politics, global events, and the stock market, are just some of the random articles located in the newspaper that always seem to change on a daily basis. No matter how similar each article can be from one day to the next, you would never see the exact same piece of information show up in the same area of the newspaper ever again. Regardless of what section of the newspaper you find to be most fulfilling or exciting, the news always seemed to change each day. That is what makes current events so outstanding; simply the fact that they always remain "current", not old.

With regards to the "sense" of current events, there are also <u>different types of information</u> that can be attached to each other in order for the readers to better understand the significance of such present-day activities. Factors such as a person's name, various locations, types of activities, and resulting consequences, are just some of the different variables that made up the essential elements of what is considered actual news. In order for an event to have actually occurred and to be reported, such event must have been related to the "actions" of a "person", as well as such event occurring in a specific place and time. Sounds a little bit familiar, don't you think?

In addition, such reportable event needs to have had some type of lasting consequence on the outside community or some other type of measurable quality that will allow the reader to better mentally define such information. As you will later see, each of these variables not only has a direct effect on the minds of the people who actually read the news, but also on how the actual event itself becomes reportable in the first place. But before we get carried away with discussing the various theories and principles regarding news reporting, let's first examine some of our previous discussions about memory and how it relates to <u>current events</u>.

Previously, in one of our chapters regarding personal information, it was discussed about how to remember numerical dates and times. Subjects such as a person's birthday or time of the day could easily be recalled by just using numbers, as well as sometimes using vocabulary words to denote the theme of the particular date. Days of the week, months, years, and daily hours could simply be delineated by using select groupings of numbers and abbreviations for such purposes. This chapter will continue to cover that lesson as well as give you some additional tips on how to best remember current events as well as historical dates, and how to categorize them.

During most of Sherlock Holmes's career, he would always take the time to read the morning newspaper each day so that he could keep up to date on what was then referred to as "*sensational literature*". In today's time, this is generally referred to as "police blotter". In addition, Holmes would also read through each day's newspaper to see if there were any relevant or historical events that had occurred somewhere in London or outside the city limits. Certain newspapers such as "The Courier",

"Daily Telegraph" and "London News" were just some of the various forms of literature that Holmes loved to use to elevate his mind each day when he was not busying himself with certain projects around the house.

Whenever he found himself out of work and with no real apparent case to work on, Sherlock would tend to socially isolate in the household as well as sleep in his pajamas for days. However, once he was presented with the morning newspaper, and had a chance to read through it, Holmes would find himself a little more energized and excited about the day. This is because he was guaranteed to find some type of information that he would find relevant to one of his former cases in each editorial. No matter what the subject of the article was about, Holmes always seemed to find some type of connection between the information that was contained in such tabloid with some other relevant case that he was already working on. In a way, he was essentially "linking" such materials between information that he already knew from the past, with new information that he was just learning at the time.

According to his biographer and best friend, Dr. Watson, Holmes seemed to have an incredible knowledge of sensational literature as opposed to most other subjects that he seemed to master. Watson used to state that Holmes appeared to have an encyclopedic knowledge about almost every type of major crime that had occurred within the streets of London for the past several decades. He would often remember the name of the individual of interest, as well as the date and location of the crime, and the various details related to such criminal act.

Despite his phenomenal gift for remembering such information so vividly, Holmes was also known to be quite gifted in various other fields of study, such as biology, chemistry and forensics. However, his greatest love was that of "sensational literature", or basically what most of us tend to read in the local police blotter, as well as other major headline news articles. It was from this particular field of interest, that Holmes was best able to effectively determine who was most likely a suspect of a former crime, and who was quite possibly a target of a future crime. It seemed as though these stories of various crimes appeared to awaken the "*senses*" within our favorite literary figure.

Holmes used to not only keep a collection of various newspapers around his less than tidy office, but he also kept clippings and pages of various news items in select folders throughout his desk drawers. At times, he would also write out certain pieces of information about specific people as well as relevant activities that were related to such persons. Time and time again, whenever he would hear the name of a certain individual whose name was considered as a person of interest, Holmes would go to his newspaper piles, or to his filing cabinet, and would then locate some materials about such person. Information such as the person's name, date of birth, title of significance, and the related crime attached to such person, were all contained within the confines of the cluttered office space of the legendary detective.

Sometimes it is hard to imagine how Holmes was capable of remembering so much information regarding the various criminal acts that had occurred through the city of London. However, if you think back to a previous lesson regarding how to create various codes for your memory images, it was discussed that in order to better remember something, you have to make it stand out or **POP** in your head. That way it is easier to recall as opposed to just remembering unimportant pieces of information. Most of us will only remember certain events that stand out in the news as opposed to other things that don't seem to be of such incredible importance to us. I guess it is true what they say; if it *bleeds* it reads.

Articles that deal with significant events, such as major victories or terrible losses, tend to stick out in our minds a lot longer than remembering the various ingredients for a certain recipe we had seen in the food column. The reason why we tend to remember such historical information so easily is because this incident tends to be very personal or influential to us. When we hear about something happening in the news that is quite momentous and unexpected, we tend to feel a certain connection or "link" with such current event, as we seem to wonder what it must have been like to have been there at the time that the event occurred.

Although we have already touched upon how to remember a specific date in history, which is usually as easy as remembering random sequences of numbers, we also have to pay attention to another concept that was discussed earlier in the book. And that concept was referred to as the **PAO method**, or the <u>Person-Action-Object method</u>. In this respect, in order to better recall current events, or historical dates, it is important to remember that in order for an event to have occurred, it must have happened either directly or indirectly due to the actions of another being or object. Things such as financial changes, sports scores, deaths, births, marriages, political events, health concerns, or just your typical average criminal act, all seem to have the same elements of a person committing an action of some type upon another person or object. No event that has ever been recorded in a newspaper or a history book can ever truly be imaginable without a person, action or object being associated with it.

In order to better understand the science behind memorizing current events and historical dates, we also have to have a classification system for what particular "events" or "dates" we are interested in memorizing. Without some type of system of categorization for such mnemonic challenges, it might seem rather difficult to accurately recall certain events from our memory if we don't actually know what the significance of such incident was really all about. In the chapter regarding personal information memory, we talked about how to remember dates of birth and death, as well as the associated images that were related to such milestones. We also talked about the various "steps" that were needed to attach specific images to each other to make them more memorable. Remember, the number 12 might have some significance when it comes to the apartment for Sherlock Holmes.

As for myself, I tend to have a list of at least **12 DIFFERENT HISTORICAL DATE IMAGES** that I chose to use when I try to remember a specific historical date or event. If you can think of any other types of categories for historical events on your own, please feel free to include them on this list and create new images at your own discretion. The list of such different historical date images that I tend to use is listed below:

TYPE OF EVENT	ASSOCIATED IMAGE
Birth	Baby crib
Death	Tombstone
Marriage	Wedding cake

Divorce	Crying children
New job or title	Large crown on head
Criminal action	Convict with ball and chain
Purchase/selling	Large wads of money
Conflict or fight	Battle scene
Creation or discovery	Chemical test tubes boiling
Idea or theory	Large lightbulb above head
Failure or loss/ending	Curtains closing on a stage
Succession or victory	Flag on top of a mountain

Now, the way this works is that there are certain "steps" that you have to follow in order to better remember historical dates or current events. The first thing you need to do is to picture the person, object or place (**POP**) that is most likely associated with the actual date itself. In order to do this, you have to try to use the Substitution Method. You will then try to imagine an image of the "name" that is associated with the person, object or place that you are trying to recall. After this, you would attach an image from the list above of the **12 historical date images** next to the original image listed for this name. Then, next to this picture, you will place a series of numbers that will signify the actual date that is relevant to this information. We have already covered how to memorize days of the week and months of the year in a previous chapter. This style is very similar to the POA method that was discussed earlier. For your convenience, I have included a diagram of what this information really looks like.

RELATED <u>NAME</u> FOR EVENT	<u>TYPE</u> OF HISTORICAL EVENT	<u>DATE</u> WHEN EVENT OCCURRED

At this point, I think it might be a good idea to include an example of such information so that you can better see how I am doing this particular mnemonic technique. Let's say that I wanted to remember the exact date of the ***death of President John F. Kennedy***. Well, the first thing that I would have to do is come up with an image that can be substituted for the *name* of such person. When I think about John

Kennedy, I can either picture what he looks like from a history book, or what does his name look like or sound like to me. I then attach this image to the first room or location in one of my memory palaces.

Next to this image, I then conjure up another image for *what type of event* I am trying to recall. In this instance, I am trying to remember his death. So I would attach a picture of a tombstone next to whatever image I have created for the name of John Kennedy. This image could be located to the right of my first image, or I could place it in the next room or location in my memory palace. And finally, next to the image of the tombstone, I would attach *a series of numbers* that would relate to the day of his death, such as month/day/year. The date of his death was November 22, 1963. So for that, I would picture the images for the numbers **11** (month of the year), **22** (day of the month) and **19 + 63** (year of the century). In this sequence, it would look like the image for the letters **AA**, having some type of interaction with the image for the letters **BB**. And then next to this 4 digit combination, I would attach an image of the letters **AN** having some type of interaction with the image for the letters **SC**.

Earlier, I showed you a diagram regarding how to combine the elements of the name of the historical event, the type of historical event, and the date associated with the historical event. I also told you about the filing system of Sherlock Holmes, and how he chose to organize his personal materials. At this point, I think it might be a good idea to introduce you to another method of mnemonic note taking that can aid you in your quest to be able to better remember historical information. Earlier in the book, we talked about a note taking method used to remember personal information, which was referred to as the **Farley File**.

In this notetaking method, I showed you how to organize various pieces of personal information about a person so that you could be able to memorize only the most important information you needed to know about such person. Well, the next method I am about to show you is a little bit different, as we are not going to be focusing on personal information, but rather information of a historical nature. And this new method of mnemonic note taking is referred to as **THE CHARTING METHOD**. Sounds quite matter of "fact", don't you think?

The **<u>Charting Method</u>** is a method of note taking that is specifically designed to help people better remember only the most pertinent or important information necessary to understand various fields of study. Subjects such as history, science, and mathematics all can be learned much easier using this particular note taking technique. In this instance, what you are really doing is only focusing on the "facts" that need to be memorized for certain information, not the related concepts or ideas behind such information. The Charting Method tends to work better when used with subjects that deal with more concrete factual information as opposed to abstract theorems and generalities.

If you are interested in remembering certain concepts such as **WHO, WHAT, WHERE, WHEN, WHY OR HOW,** then the <u>Charting Method</u> is the best method for completing such activity. You are going to be shortening the amount of information that you want to memorize, but by doing so in a certain order and function. Realize that there is no one specific way to use the format of the <u>Charting Method</u>, much like there is no one particular way to use the Farley File. In either case, it just depends upon what "types" of information you are interested in memorizing, as well as what individual pieces of information you find to be most important to memorize.

Before I give you an illustration of such technique, let's return to the previous example of historical memory. I spoke with you earlier about remembering a specific historical date, which included *the death of former President John F. Kennedy on November 22, 1963*. In that instance, I showed you how to remember his name, the type of event that occurred to him (death), and the date that was associated with it. Well, let's say that you wanted to remember the actual location where his death occurred (<u>where</u>), as well as the specific manner in which his death happened (<u>why</u>), and the context of events in which his death took place (<u>how</u>). In this case, after you have created images for the main character's first and last name (name), the next piece of information that you would attach would be the images for what had actually happened to such person (death). Then next to these images, you would insert another series of images that were related to the dates of the historical event (day/month/year).

Well, as you already know, this information was already covered.

Now, let's take it a step further. Following the date of the historical event, you would then place another series of images in another location of your memory palace that were related to the location of where the historical event occurred. Earlier, we talked about how to memorize personal information about other people. We discussed how to create images for addresses and locations, based upon numbers memory and the substitution method for words. Well, President Kennedy died on November 22, 1963 in Dallas, Texas. In this case, you would create images for both the name of the town (Dallas), and the state that it occurred in (Texas). Feel free to use whatever images you would prefer for such instance, as long as the images look like, sound like, or remind you of both the city and state.

After these images are transposed into your memory palace, you will now want to be able to recall the manner in which the historical event occurred, or in this case *WHY* did President Kennedy die. As you might remember from reading US history, Kennedy died as a result of being shot by a bullet fired from a gun. So, with that information in mind, you will try to create an image for a bullet coming out of a gun in the next location in your memory palace. Since this is a very graphic and disturbing picture to imagine, it will be easy to conjure up some images that can be related to such manner of death.

And finally, the last thing you might want to recall is the context in which the historical event occurred (how). On that particular date, the President was shot while riding in the backseat of his car, sitting alongside his wife. And with that in mind, you would create images of a large car with people sitting in the back seat, and place it in the last location in your memory palace. This is a very easy image to create as most of us are familiar with what a car looks like, as well as where backseat passengers usually sit. And there you have it; you have just memorized the exact chronological information related to one of the most historic events of the 20th century in the US.

Now, while that might seem like a lot of information to memorize for just one particular historical event, it can actually be quite easy to do so once you only focus on the basic facts that you want to memorize. Below I have included an example template for using the <u>Charting Method of Note taking</u>, and I have filled in the information related to the previous historical event regarding John Kennedy. I will discuss such method of note taking in greater detail in a later chapter. Just remember, there is no particular way to use the Charting Method, as different subjects require different pieces of information that need to be memorized in order to recall the subject matter at hand. But in this instance, since we are talking about both current and historical events, we will only be focusing on the previously discussed elements such as **WHO, WHAT, WHERE, WHEN, WHY and HOW.**

WHO	WHAT	WHERE	WHEN	WHY	HOW
President John Kennedy	Death	Dallas, Texas	November 22, 1963	Shot by bullet	While sitting in back of car next to wife
Related image	Related image	Related image	Related image	Related image	Related image

But don't worry; I am not going to quiz you on how to use the Charting Method in regards to any future memory tests for historical dates. The reason why I chose not to quiz you on this technique is because *there is no one way to actually use this note taking technique.* Therefore everyone is free to use it in a different way. However, I will be giving you a memory test on <u>historical dates</u> based upon the concept of **PAO,** or Person Action Object. For this memory quiz, we are going to be focusing on **7 historical events that occurred during the time of Sherlock Holmes.** While these dates might be considered historical to many of us living in the 21st century, they were more considered current events during the time of Sherlock Holmes. And not only will I be expecting you to memorize the historical data presented to you, I will also be giving you a few quiz questions to answer in order to see how well you were able to conceptualize such information.

First, before you begin this next exercise, you will need at least two pieces of paper. On one sheet of paper, you will be using this one to <u>write down</u> the historical information exactly as it is written. Feel free to either use cursive or print, whichever is easiest for you to read. Make sure that you put down the correct information that is presented to you on this sheet of paper, so that you can recall the information as needed. Each historical event will have a number attached to it, as each event is a separate entity to be memorized. Once you are done writing down all of the historical information, turn this paper over and don't look at it. Next, take out a second piece of paper. This piece of paper will be used as your answer sheet. On this sheet of piece, create several small tables which look like the previous example of PAO memory, which is included below.

RELATED NAME FOR EVENT	TYPE OF HISTORICAL EVENT	DATE WHEN EVENT OCCURRED

After you have created each small table, include a number next to each one, so that you have enough space to fill in all of the information. Next, on the *bottom* of this paper, please write down all the related quiz questions that I have listed, as well as numbering them correctly. They will include questions regarding historical names, types of events, and the dates associated with certain events, as well as some analyzing questions. Leave some space between all of the tables and the questions, so that you not only have enough room to fill out each table individually, but also to answer each question. Finally, once you have completed all of your related PAO tables and have written down the entire list of quiz questions; put this piece of paper away. Take a minute or two to try to relax and go over your memory palaces, as well as any related images that you might want to use to later recall such information.

Make sure that you have a watch or a timer with you, so that you can keep track of your time for this exercise. Once you feel ready to begin, flip over the first piece of paper with the historical events on it, and begin to memorize all of the materials that were presented to you. In this case, you will be given **15 MINUTES** to memorize all of the related historical information. If you finish earlier than expected, just write down your times so that you know how long it took you to complete it. After your time is up, or after you have memorized all of the historical events, flip this piece of paper back over so that you cannot see it.

Give yourself several minutes to review the information in your head, go back and check your memory palaces if needed. When you feel confident that you have gone over the information enough, take out the second piece of paper, and first begin to write out all of the information in the tables in a <u>PAO fashion</u> for each historical date. Then, once you have completed this particular task, look down at the bottom of your paper to see the related quiz questions. From the information that you have filled in through your PAO tables, try to answer as many of the related questions as you can. It seems as though you will have to "switch" from memorizing information to answering related questions.

For this exercise, you will have to be able to recall **21 SEPARATE PIECES OF HISTORICAL INFORMATION**, as well as to be able to correctly answer **12 REVIEW QUESTIONS**. Notice how the numbers are "switched" from one to the other. That means that for each piece of information you recall correctly, or for each question you get right, you can give yourself <u>3.3 points</u>. Spelling does count, so try to make sure that you are careful about how certain names and locations are spelled. Once you are done filling in all of the PAO information, and answering all of the related questions, go back and flip over the first sheet of paper, which has all of the original information written down on it. Make sure that it matches what was written in the book. Go back and check to see how well you did.

This might be a daunting task to complete, but it is good practice if you want to be able to learn how to better memorize historic information or current events, no matter what time period you live in. If you don't do well on this exercise at first, do not be too upset. Take a day off from this exercise, and then go back and try it again in the same fashion, and see how well you did the next time. You will begin to notice that after you have practiced it a few times, the information will start to become easier to memorize at a later date. Well, good luck and remember that, when it comes to historical information, Sherlock would state, "There is nothing more deceptive than an obvious fact".

<u>SHERLOCK HOLMES HISTORICAL DATES</u>

1. PRINCE ALBERT/ DIES/ DECEMBER 14, 1861
2. QUEEN VICTORIA/ CROWNED/ JUNE 20, 1837
3. SLAVERY/ ENDS/ AUGUST 1, 1838
4. LONDON SUBWAY/ OPENS/ JANUARY 9, 1863

5. PENNY POST STAMP/ CREATED/ JANUARY 10, 1840
6. JACK THE RIPPER/ FINAL
MURDER/ NOVEMBER 8, 1889
7. CRIMEAN WAR/ BATTLE/ MARCH 28, 1854

REVIEW QUESTIONS:

1. What happened on November 8, 1889?
2. When did the London Subway first open up?
3. What ended on August 1st, 1838?
4. When was the penny post stamp created?
5. What occurred on March 28th, 1854?
6. When did Prince Albert die?
7. What major event occurred on June 20th, 1837?
8. The London Subway opened, and the penny stamps were both created during what month of the year?
9. What event occurred first in the timeline?
10. What event occurred last in the timeline?
11. Which came first, the end of slavery or the crowning of Queen Victoria?
12. From the 1830's through the 1880's, what decade was NOT included in this timeline?

DAY EXERCISE	SCORE (PERCENT/ CORRECT)	TIME (MINUTES, SECOND)
FIRST DAY		
SECOND DAY		
THIRD DAY		
FOURTH DAY		
FIFTH DAY		
SIXTH DAY		
SEVENTH DAY		

AVERAGE SCORE=

AVERAGE TIME=

CHAPTER 10

THE "WOMAN'S" TOUCH (HOUSEHOLD MEMORY)

For most of us, walking around our household during the day is something that we do quite naturally. After we have lived in the same residence for a certain period of time, we often get so comfortable with our natural surroundings that we tend to stop paying attention to all of the little details around us. For anybody who has ever purchased a new home, you are quite aware of the feelings that you had when you first walked through each and every room in such house. You also realized that you were free to decorate or refurbish each room in whatever manner you chose to do so. That is one of the greatest things about moving into a new residence. Each room is virtually a clean slate that is waiting for you to give it some color, or in some cases, a "woman's touch".

In any typical home, there are usually <u>6 different types of rooms</u> that are found within any family size house. These rooms are used for variously different purposes for any residents that are either living in such location or have just come to visit. The types of rooms that you are most likely to see in a regular family household are the following: **bedrooms, bathrooms, living room, kitchen, dining room and guest room**. However, there are many households out there that have other types of rooms that are not included on this list. Sometimes people will turn the living room into a TV room, other times the guest room can be used for storage. Either way, there is a chance that if you live in any given house, or go to visit someone else's home; you will probably notice most of these different types of household rooms at some point in your "journey".

Each room carries with it a different purpose as well as a different expectation for how the room is supposed to look. For most of us, the living room usually seems to be the largest room in the house, and the bathroom tends to be the smallest room in the household. The bedrooms usually appear to be located on the upper floors of each house, while the kitchen and dining room tends to be found on the lower floor of each house. Sometimes you will find an attic and a basement located in such residence, although both rooms tend to not have many guests walking through them. All in all, no matter what house you end up walking through, each experience is like a journey through a "palace", in of itself. I have created a small rubric that I tend to use to memorize the names of each of these household rooms, feel free to create whatever images you would prefer or to add any additional rooms or names to this list.

NAME OF ROOM	ASSOCIATED IMAGE
Bedroom	Large bed
Bathroom	Giant tub
Living Room	Sofa or couch
Kitchen	Stove or refrigerator
Dining Room	Large table
Guest Room	Vacancy sign

One of the reasons why I chose to focus on this area of memory is because it is something that most of us are not trained to pay attention to in our daily lives. Yet it remains something that is vitally pertinent to our activities of daily living. We cannot live without being inside of a residential structure, as many of us would not survive long outdoors in the wilderness. And yet, no matter how many times you walk through your household during your lifetime, many of us are guilty of not remembering many details about our surrounding domestic environments. Whether it is remembering how many steps lead up to the second floor, or how many lights are located in each room, most of us are just too comfortable to not really "observe" what lies in front of us. This is a subject matter that we are going to explore in a different way in a future chapter, but for now, let's try to focus on how to improve your **HOUSEHOLD MEMORY**.

Throughout most of his journeys, Sherlock Holmes was able to outwit and outsmart many of his adversaries, colleagues, and even his friends. Even with his genius intellect and superhuman deductive abilities, it seemed as though nobody was powerful enough to get the best over our beloved super sleuth. However, there was only one person, or more specifically, one "woman" who was able to outmaneuver and manipulate Holmes in such a way that he was unable to predict what her next move was going to be.

One of the most famous supporting characters in the history of the Sherlock Holmes franchise was a woman named **_Irene Adler_**. She was a noted con artist, debutante, musician, and sometimes faithful companion to Sherlock Holmes. She used her beauty and her charm, as well as her charisma and social skills, to distract Holmes just when he was getting close to either solving a case, or determining what new tricks she had up her sleeve. Although she only showed up in a few of his many stories, she was always referenced after the fact by Holmes throughout several of his future journeys. And instead of calling her by her full name, he would often refer to her as "the woman". That is quite a fitting sentiment to the one that truly "got away".

As far as **household memory** is concerned, nobody else out there was better able to memorize the layout of a particular room than Sherlock Holmes. Whether it was the number of books on a shelf, the type of flowers on a counter, or even the placement of a rug on the floor, Sherlock was always able to observe his surroundings in such a way that if even one item was moved out of place, he was certain to have taken notice of it. In one of his final stories, "The Second Stain", Sherlock later walks into a crime scene where he notices that the rug on the floor has been moved. Despite the fact that he had been in the room just once before, he did take notice of the exact location of this particular rug. And when returning again to the same room on a different day, he immediately realizes that this particular item is not in its usual place. This eventually leads him to realize that a key piece of evidence may have been effected by this subtle yet noticeable movement of this one particular fabric.

In another instance, Sherlock is able to remember a particular decoration that he saw in a room much earlier. He then is able to relate to others why he feels that this one special article is so important to his overall case. In one of his many adventures, Sherlock is walking through a room that is full of lots of books on different subjects. He also sees that there are numerous plants and flowers located near several of the windows. One innocuously looking book that he seems to pay attention to is a book that discusses the topic of gardening and flowers. He also notices that this book appears as though it has been touched or handled in a certain way that signifies that its reader had previous contact with it before.

While this might not seem as much a huge astonishment to most people reading this story, Sherlock also realizes that many of the flowers in the room are dying due to lack of water. He then deduces that whoever has been reading this particular book is someone who is either not familiar with gardening, or perhaps is someone who is missing from the room. By this, I mean that he knows that if someone were to be interested in the topic of gardening, that particular individual would have read such book and then paid more attention to the care and maintenance of the flowers in the surrounding area. From this one particular act of memorizing household items, Holmes is able to come one step closer to finding out who the real criminal is in this particular case.

The ability to memorize the layout of a room as well as the various features located within is a skill that most investigators and police detectives are highly trained in. This does not mean that other people in the world are not able to have the same abilities and talents as these unique professionals. It is just that in their lines of work, they are required to walk into an unfamiliar room, and then try to take notice of various objects that are not in their proper locations. Although no one room in the world is ever perfect, there are certain "expectations" for each room that most of these special individuals are acutely aware of when they enter such locations. Sometimes noticing even the smallest details can make the biggest difference when it comes to gathering the evidence needed to locate the guilty parties of such numerous crimes.

There is another instance where Holmes has to find out what key piece of evidence Irene Adler is hiding in order to help save the reputation of one of his higher-ranking colleagues. In "A Scandal in Bohemia", Holmes has arrived at the location where Irene Adler is currently staying. He has enough time to walk through the entire room and pay attention to all of the hidden details of this particular location. He then realizes that such evidence will not be easy to find in this special case. His friend John Watson is able to create a small fire in such room, resulting in lots of smoke and ash to permeate throughout the building.

In this instance, Adler runs over to a hidden protective panel on the wall and then collects certain valuables from inside. She then later takes these items with her before Holmes is able to stop her. He later returns to this room the next day, and goes to the very same location where he suspects that she must have hid such valuables. Unfortunately, by the time he gets there he realizes that he was too late to stop her. However, he then later surprises his friends and colleagues by making an astonishing revelation. He states that he was already aware that such evidence had to have been hidden in such location, as this would have been the first place where such a woman would go if she were afraid that her valuables were to be destroyed. It is very likely that she herself had previously rearranged the room in such a way before Sherlock even knew the outlay of each piece of furniture. In this way, she had given the room a "woman's touch" so that she could outsmart Holmes in this particular situation.

And for that reason, I am going to give you a particular method that I have come up with which helps to be better able to memorize household items. And that method is referred to as the **ADLER METHOD.** In this instance, the name **ADLER** is spelled with five different letters. Each letter relates to a different concept that is relevant to the study of the outlines of a room. This word in of itself is a type of mnemonic that can be used by people who want to be able to better organize how they go about memorizing the items in a particular household. And once you understand what each of the letters of the term "ADLER" stands for, you will have a better idea about why this particular mnemonic is so effective when it comes to memorizing household rooms. The definition of the **ADLER METHOD** is listed below:

A= Articles or accessories
D= Decorations or decorum
L= Lighting locations
E= Exits and Entrances
R= Repairs or renovation

To start off, in the ADLER method, the first letter is the letter "A", which stands for <u>articles, or accessories</u>. In this instance, when you first walk into a room, pay attention to what types of <u>articles</u> of furniture, or other related <u>accessories</u> that are located in such area. Things such as beds, chairs, couches, dressers, tables, counters, shelves, sinks, and desks, are just some of the items that you will find in many rooms throughout a house. Other items such as TV, computer, or musical items can easily be imagined in your mind as well. Each item serves a different purpose for each room that it is placed in. And each item will probably be located in a particular arrangement when compared to other items in the room.

In the ADLER method, this is probably the most time consuming step to take out of all of the other letters. The best thing to do in order to memorize the layout of a particular room is to take notice of **HOW MANY OF,** and **WHAT COLOR** each item of furniture is. We already covered how to memorize numbers and colors in some of our previous chapters. However, what we did not cover was how to memorize the actual items in a room in of itself.

For this chapter, I have created a rubric so that I can better accomplish such objective. Instead of actually memorizing the word "bed", I chose to create a code for such basic furniture. In this example, the word "bed" becomes the letters "BD", as these are the letters most commonly associated with such word. And for the word "chair", I chose to use the letters "CH" so that I don't get it confused with anything else. You are free to make up your own images or letter codes for each piece of furniture that you might encounter. However, for this chapter of memory, I have included a small chart that I tend to use in order to better encode images for remembering furniture. These are the **10 MOST COMMON ARTICLES OF FURNITURE** that are found in most household rooms. If you can think of any other types of articles of furniture based upon your own experiences, please feel free to create images for such reasons.

HOUSEHOLD ITEM	ASSOCIATED LETTER IMAGES
Bed	BD= images for letters B and D
Chair	CH= images for letters C and H
Couch	CC- images for letters C and C
Cabinet	CB= images for letter C and B
Dresser	DS= images for letters D and S
Table	AB= images for letters A and B
Counter	CO= images for letters C and O
Shelf	SH= images for letters S and H
Sink	SN= images for letters S and N
Desk	DK= images for letters D and E

The reason why I chose to use letter combinations instead of simply picturing the actual piece of furniture is because trying to memorize furniture can be quite confusing when you are using the Memory Palace technique. Earlier, when we talked about how to use the Memory Palace technique, you were told to mentally walk around a room and try to notice the different items or locations that most likely grabbed your attention. No matter what houses or palaces you chose to use for your various memory journeys, it is most likely that if you are trying to use one particular room in any one of your memory palaces, you will probably chose to use random pieces of furniture as different locations to store information for your memory purposes.

Earlier in one of the first chapters of the book, I talked to you about how to use the outline of one of the rooms in my house as an example of a memory palace. There were various things that were located in this particular room, such as couches, tables and shelves. If you wanted to use the previous example of my personal room in order to memorize the layout of the furniture in your own home, it might get confusing for you. You would need to try to actually picture each piece of furniture, and then attach such item to the various locations that I previously labeled for my own room. In the previous example, the first location in my own personal room was a TV set, as this was the first location in one of my memory palaces.

For this instance, if you wanted to attach an image for a "bed" to the location of the TV set that I previously described, you might actually confuse yourself into thinking that that particular "bed" was supposed to be located in this particular memory palace room. This would not be unexpected in the most cases. Therefore, instead of actually picturing furniture, it is best to create a "substitute" image for each of piece of furniture. That way you don't get confused in the future for such reasons. Also, when picturing things like a TV, computer or musical related equipment, simply just create an image for such appliance and place it in the same room of your memory palace.

The next step to focus on is to count how many of each type of piece of furniture you notice in a certain location. Normally, you will only find one or two beds in a particular room. But there is a chance that you might find numerous chairs, desks, or counters in various rooms. Therefore, it is important to make sure that you take a few moments and try to count the exact number of each type of furniture that you see in the room. You already know how to create images for numbers 00-99. In this case, you will probably only have to use single digits, so try to use images for items such as OA, OB, OC, etc.

Therefore, if I notice that a particular room has 4 dressers in it, I would create a series of images as follow: OD and DS. In this case, the number 04 would be represented by OD, and the image for a "dresser" would be represented by the letter DS. This is a particularly easy image to recall, and I can place it in any one of my memory palaces. In the end, you will more than likely only have to create images for a pair of two letter combinations, such as what was listed before. The first two letters would signify a number, and the next two letters would signify the type of furniture. From my previous list of codes, this is an easy image to conjure up.

After counting the number of different pieces of furniture for each room, the next step to take is to pay attention to what color such pieces of furniture are. Most times, in many houses, one chair will be the same color as another chair. One dresser will be the same color as another dresser. And one shelf will be the same color as another shelf. This tends to be the way that most households are decorated as most people tend to like conformity in their color choices at home, as opposed to multiple colors on various pieces of furniture. And we already covered how to memorize various colors of the rainbow in a previous chapter.

You are free to create as many different images for as many colors as you would like, even if you are not an interior decorator. So, in the previous example, if I noticed that there were 4 dressers in one particular room, and that all of the dressers were brown in color, then I could picture the following image: <u>OD and DS, and an image for the color "brown"</u>. In this case, I would create images of the letter combinations of OD and DS, and then follow that with an image for the color "brown". And I would place this series of images in the first location of one of my memory palaces.

As far as the next letter in the ADLER method, the letter "D" stands for <u>decorations</u> or the <u>decorum</u> of the room. For the most part, the number of decorations in a particular room is more than likely going to be larger than the number of pieces of furniture in a particular room. Usually in most households, there are usually **5 DIFFERENT TYPES OF DECORATIONS** that one will see scattered around on the walls, or on top of various pieces of furniture. The 5 most common types of decorations that you will likely see in any given room are: <u>pictures, paintings, clocks, sculptures and personal relics</u>. If you can think of any other types of decorations that would normally be present in most rooms throughout a household, please feel free to create whatever images you would like for such purposes.

Usually, not all of these items will have the same color. Most likely some will have multiple colors for each object. In this case, you will only have to memorize how many of each time of item that you see in a particular room, as opposed to having to remember all of the various colors associated with each item. However, there have been times when I have walked into a room, and have noticed numerous pieces of the same type of decoration in any one particular area. As for me personally, I had a very special party held one time in a banquet room with over 100 clocks lined against the walls. I knew that I would never be able to count that many clocks in a single day while trying to socialize with my guests. Therefore, if the number of each type of decoration in a room is simply too large to count in just a few seconds, simply give an estimate as to how many you think you see in such room.

In regards to coming up with images for these five types of decorations, simply conjure up an image that is easy to recall that can be associated with each type of decoration. However, be careful when using these images if you have already elected to use them in your own personal memory palaces. If I wanted to create an image for a "picture", I can easily imagine an old large camera. If I wanted to create an image for a "painting", I would create an image for the Mona Lisa. All that you would need to do is attach an image for the actual number of each type of decoration to the image of the decoration itself. So, if the room that I entered had 8 different pictures hanging from the walls, I would create an image for the letters OH and then attach this to the image of an old large camera. And then finally, I would attach this image to the next location in one of my memory palaces. Also, don't forget to pay attention to what *colors* can be found on the walls of such room, as this is considered "decorum". Simply create an image for the word "wall" and then attach an image for the corresponding color that you are associating with such. This can also go in the same room of your memory palace.

With regards to the third letter in the ADLER method, the letter "L" stands for lighting. This is generally one of the easiest steps in the ADLER method. In this case, all that you need to do is to be able to count how "many" light fixtures you see in such a room. However, remember that sometimes a room will only have lights coming from the ceiling. In other rooms, the lights are situated on side tables. For this step, simply try to count out the actual number of lights in a room, and use your previous number codes to attach an image for such. When I think about an image for a light, I always think of a "lightbulb", but you are free to create whatever images you would like. So, if I walk into a room and it has 3 different lights in different locations, I would remember the number 03 as **OC,** and then I would attach that image to the image of a lightbulb. I would then store such combinations of images in a third location or room in one of my memory palaces.

Another easy letter to utilize in the ADLER method is the letter "E", which stands for <u>entrances</u> and <u>exits</u>. For this part of the ADLER method, it is important to consider not only what doors are leading into a room, but also what other doors can be used to get into the next adjoining room. Sometimes, you will walk into a room with only one door, so there is only one entrance and exit. Other times, you will find yourself in a room with doors that lead into closets or storage places, which cannot be used for exits. These too need to be considered for such category. And finally, there are many rooms where there is usually one door used to enter such room, and another door used to exit into the adjoining room.

For this part of the ADLER method, all you have to do is simply count the number of doors in total for such room, and create an image for such number. Then attach an image for the word "door" next to such numerical image, and store this in the next location in your memory palace. For example, if the room I am entering has one door leading into it, one door leading into another room, and one closet door, then it would total three doors or the letters **OC**. This would then be followed by the image of the word "door", which you are free to create whatever image you want for such reasons.

Finally, the last letter in the ADLER method is the letter "R", which stands for <u>repairs or renovations</u>. Usually, this is only to be used if the room that you are entering appears as though there has been some type of reconstruction that was previously done. **The 5 MOST COMMON TYPES OF REPAIRS OR RENOVATIONS** that are usually seen in most rooms are<u>: plumbing, electrical, flooring, painting, and construction.</u> If you can think of any other types of renovations or repairs, go ahead and create images for such. Don't be surprised if most of the rooms that you walk into will not have any of these changes occurring in them. Most homeowners do not want other people walking into rooms of their houses that are not completely finished. If the room that you walk into has no major renovations or repairs, simply just skip this step entirely.

However, if you do find yourself entering into such room for any reasons, simply try to take notice of any major types of work being done. Then create an image for any of these different types of renovations. For instance, the term "plumbing" conjures up an image of Super Mario, as this image reminds me of a plumber. You don't have to have any expert knowledge of home repairs or maintenance for such purposes. Feel free to create whatever images you want if you can recognize what type of handiwork is being done. But for this instance, simply create an image for whatever type of renovations or repairs are being done. Then place this image in the last location in your memory palace. And there you have it; you have just memorized the entire layout of a room using the **ADLER method**.

One trick that I tend to use when applying such method to the memorization of an actual room is to mentally prepare myself for the future task of memorizing such materials. For this, I will usually repeat the name "ADLER" to myself before I enter a new room that I have never been in before. I also make sure that I spell out the actual word ADLER, one letter at a time quietly to myself. This will allow me to mentally prepare my mind to be able to organize all of the future materials without feeling too overwhelmed or confused.

Another skill that I use when applying this method is to walk into a room that I am already familiar with, and try to time myself to see how long it takes for me to be able to accomplish the entire ADLER technique. Sometimes, I will be able to go through all of the five different letters of the ADLER method in just a few minutes. Other times I will be able to accomplish this task in just a few seconds. It all depends on much material is currently present inside of the room that I am entering. The more items that I see in any particular room will affect how long it takes for me to completely memorize them.

Just for starters, the best advise that I can give you, in regards to how to practice such technique, is to walk over to any major room in your home or residence that you would prefer. Then, when you enter such room, repeat to yourself the name **ADLER**, and make sure that you spell it out one letter at a time. After this, look around the room in a full circle or walk around if needed. Take in all of the materials that you see before you. Go through each letter, one at a time; do not try to skip a letter as this might confuse you later on during your recall. Make sure that you count out all of the items that you see for each letter, as well as any related descriptors for each type of article.

Once you have created images for all of the information for each letter in the ADLER method, go back and review such information again in your head. After you feel that you have completed this exercise completely, walk out of the room and close the door. Next, take out a piece of paper and write down the following questions to yourself. I have listed **8 questions** below that you will need to answer correctly in order to master this exercise. Don't worry about adding up any points for this exercise; just try to see how many questions you can fully answer. This is your first real attempt at using this method. Once you are done answering the questions, go back into the room and see how many questions you actually got right. The questions that I have listed for you are as follows:

1. **What different types of furniture did you notice in such room?**
2. **What colors were the various pieces of furniture?**
3. **What different types of decorations did you see in such room?**
4. **How many decorations did you actually notice?**
5. **What colors were the walls or ceiling?**
6. **How many lights were present in such room?**
7. **How many different doors were located in such room?**
8. **What if any types of renovations or repairs did you notice?**

After this, go to another room in your house and try the same exercise again. Make sure that you keep track of what areas of the ADLER method that you seem to struggle with the most. This will be the type of information that you will want to work on improving for future references. Try to get familiar with how to identify certain items or articles in various rooms, so that in the future you are better able to recognize such distinctions in different locations. You don't have to become an interior decorator or a home appraiser in order to become fluent at this. Just simply knowing the difference between various items is good enough for this particular field of memory improvement. I can tell the difference between a table and a chair, but I would not know the difference between a closet and a vanity.

For the last part of this chapter, I will be giving you an exercise that you can do on your own without having to walk around your own house in order to practice such method. Below, I have included a chart of a fictional house with **6 DIFFERENT ROOMS,** with different items located in each of the rooms. The rooms are listed based upon the title that is given for each room. In this exercise, I have created a chart below of all of the fictional items located in each room. For this memory challenge, you will need two pieces of paper. On your first sheet of paper, please write down the information that is presented to you exactly as it is written. Make sure that you try to create a table or a chart that looks similar to what is printed. Once you have written out all of the information, flip over your first sheet of paper so that you cannot see it. Here is the information for the fictional house.

Bedroom	Guest Room	Bathroom	Kitchen	Dining Room	Living Room
1 brown bed	1 purple couch	1 white sink	1 black table	1 brown table	1 red couch
3 tan dressers	3 blue chairs	1 blue toilet	4 grey cabinet	6 tan chairs	2 desks
2 pictures	1 clock	1 personal item	2 clocks	3 paintings	2 pictures
1 painting	2 sculptures	2 pictures	2 paintings	2 sculptures	1 personal item
White walls	Blue walls	Grey Walls	Yellow Walls	Green walls	White Walls
3 lights	2 lights	1 light	4 lights	1 light	3 lights
2 doors	1 door	1 door	3 doors	2 doors	4 doors
No repairs	construction	plumbing	Electrical	painting	No repairs

On your second sheet of paper, please write out the <u>previous 8 questions</u> that were listed on the previous page. Make sure that you put these questions on the far left hand corner of the page, and put this in one column. Then, create 6 different columns for the rest of the page, each with the label of each room that is presented. If you need to see the original questions again, here they are;

- **What different types of furniture did you notice in such room?**
- **What colors were the various pieces of furniture?**
- **What different types of decorations did you see in such room?**
- **How many decorations did you actually notice?**
- **What colors were the walls?**

- **How many lights were present in such room?**
- **How many different doors were located in such room?**
- **What if any types of renovations or repairs did you notice?**

When you are done writing out the original eight questions as well as the 6 different columns for the various household rooms on your second page, it should look similar to the diagram below:

	Bedroom	Guest Room	Bathroom	Kitchen	Dining room	Living room
Question 1						
Question 2						
Question 3						
Question 4						
Question 5						
Question 6						
Question 7						
Question 8						

At this point, take a moment to mentally prepare yourself by going through the locations in your memory palace that you wish to use, as well as any related codes for the previously listed items. You will be given **10 MINUTES TO MEMORIZE** all of the information that was listed for your first page. When you are ready, flip over the first piece of paper and start to memorize as much of the information as you can. Once you are done memorizing, or if your time runs out, simply flip this piece of paper over again so that you cannot look at it. Give yourself about <u>10 minutes</u> to review the information in your head that you have just memorized. Make sure that you have a watch or a timer for such reasons.

At this point, locate the second piece of paper with the answer diagram listed previously. Answer each question for each room by writing out the responses in whole. Make sure that you give yourself enough space to fill in all of the information as needed. Try to give yourself **15 MINUTES** to <u>write out all of your responses</u> in full. After you have completely finished putting in all of your answers, go back and flip over the first sheet of information. Check to see how many questions you answered correctly. Any miscounts or misspellings will be considered as incorrect answers. Putting the wrong information for the wrong room also counts as a mistake.

Since there are **54 pieces of information** to memorize (including the names of the rooms) give yourself <u>1.75 points</u> for each piece of information that was correct. You might need a calculator for this one exercise, as this is an odd number. And if you completed the memorization in less than 10 minutes, give yourself an extra 5 points as well. Try this once and see how well you did. And if you want to, put it away and try it again throughout the week to see if you can improve your scores. Don't' worry if this exercise causes you any stress or pressure, for as Sherlock would say, "A man always finds it hard to realize that he may have finally lost a *woman's* love, however badly he may have treated her'.

DAY EXERCISE	SCORE (PERCENT/ CORRECT)	TIME (MINUTES, SECOND)
FIRST DAY		
SECOND DAY		
THIRD DAY		
FOURTH DAY		
FIFTH DAY		
SIXTH DAY		
SEVENTH DAY		

AVERAGE SCORE=

AVERAGE TIME=

CHAPTER 11

BELL'S ANATOMY (MEDICAL MEMORY)

The human body is perhaps one of the most fascinating and complex organisms that has ever existed on this planet. Many of us simply do not take the time to truly appreciate how unique and multifaceted our bodies really are due to the fact that we don't completely understand how our own bodies work. Even for those who practice medicine every day, most of them are in awe of the spectacular nature of the human body. Even when we think we know everything there is to know about the field of medicine, we find something else out there that is new about the wonderful specimen that is the human body.

Although I am not going to be teaching you any lessons about how to practice medicine, I am going to educate you about how to memorize information about the human body and why it is important to know such information. Things like diagnostics and assessments of a medical nature should be left only to licensed professionals who have years of experience in such areas. It would be dangerous to allow you to assume that you can make accurate deductions about a person's medical nature simply based upon the lessons learned in this chapter.

The field of medicine itself is a vastly interesting and expansive field. Throughout the years, as we continue to learn more and more about the human body and related diseases, our repertoire of medical knowledge also seems to increase at an exponentially large rate. Years ago, when I was younger, there were certain ailments and comorbidities that were usually serious and untreatable. Now of days, we have more medicines and treatments available that allow us to not only reduce many of our related medical symptoms, but in some cases to actually cure certain diseases and disorders as well.

It is really quite interesting to realize just how far we have come in the past several decades with regards to the advancement of medicine. For most of us in this world, we are merely patients and consumers of such advancements in technology and bio-chemistry. When we get sick or injured, we usually look to medical professionals to help relieve our physical stresses and alleviate our sufferings. However, there are a lucky few people out there who are fortunate enough to serve as the actual providers of such ever-changing medicinal care. Their knowledge and skills allow them to be able to provide the appropriate and necessary care to those out there who are struggling with their own individual health related difficulties.

One such privileged individual was the loyal and heroic side kick of the legendary brilliant detective; Dr. John Watson. For those of you not familiar with the character of John Watson, we were first introduced to him in the first story of the Sherlock Holmes series, "A Study in Scarlet". Watson is a former British Army doctor, who had previously studied medicine in London in 1878, and eventually trained as an assistant surgeon in the British Army. He joined British forces in India, saw service in the Second Anglo-Afghan War, was wounded in battle in July 1880 by a bullet, and was later discharged the following year. He eventually found himself living back in London again, without much contact from his family. During such time, he was looking for a possible roommate who would be willing to take him in. It was at that time that he was initially introduced to his future partner in crime, and best friend, Sherlock Holmes.

During their first encounter, Holmes noticed several distinguishing features about Watson as they were first introduced to each other while visiting in a medical school laboratory. Holmes paid strict attention to the physical details and mannerisms of Watson upon their first meeting. In less than a minute of observing him, Holmes is able to deduce several things about Watson that he himself did not mention to others. By taking notice of Watson's limp, his dark tan features, and his expression of being in pain, as well as his postures and bodily mannerisms, Sherlock is able to deduce that Watson was a British Army doctor who was wounded in combat overseas, and is now trying to adjust to life back home in London, by delivering his previously mentioned infamous phrase *"You have been in Afghanistan, I perceive"*.

Watson is stunned by this remarkable display of ingenuity as well as extraordinary observational assessment. He later asks Holmes how he came to know such information about him without asking him first. Holmes then explains to Watson what he himself had noticed and observed during their first moments together in that infamous scene at the medical school. At this point, Watson is intrigued by Holmes and is willing to become not only his new roommate, but also his biographer and his partner in crime fighting. And with that, a legendary partnership first began between two different yet equally memorable characters that would later redefine the history of the 19th century literary detective genre.

There were times when Sherlock Holmes himself would try to learn various skills in the field of medicine, albeit in somewhat rudimentary or old fashioned ways. Most of these lessons would occur while he was conducting make-shift autopsies on various crime victims throughout London. Sometimes he would conduct such investigations alone in the morgue, other times he would call upon the assistance of his medically knowledgeable friend Dr. Watson to assist him in such ways.

However, none of the medical assessments that he performed on the numerous cadavers brought before him, would ever be considered ethical or legal by any means to this day. Certain activities, such as burning the hair of a body to see what color the flame would produce, to physically hitting the flesh of a corpse with a riding crop to determine what types of bruise patterns would occur on the decaying flesh, were just some of the unusual yet brilliant strategies displayed by our medical novice, Sherlock Holmes. However, when it comes to the creation of Sherlock Holmes, medicine was quite an integral part of his initial genesis. In other words, when people think about the character of Sherlock Holmes, the subject of medicine should indeed sound familiar, or in this case, should ring a "bell".

There was a very famous physician who during that time had a huge influence over the creation of the character known as Sherlock

Holmes. As many historians have explained, the author of Sherlock Holmes was a man named Sir Arthur Conan Doyle. Arthur Conan Doyle had not originally wanted to become an author of detective literature. In fact, before he became a world famous author, Doyle had initially embarked upon a career in medicine. While he was a young man, he was accepted into medical school in Edinburgh, where he wanted to eventually become a surgeon. During his time in medical school, Arthur Conan Doyle would go on to meet a man who would later change the very course of his life. And that man was none other than his medical advisor, **the legendary Dr. Joseph Bell**.

Dr. Joseph Bell was a Scottish surgeon and lecturer at the medical school at the University of Edinburgh in the 19th century. At first, Arthur Conan Doyle did not always have the closest relationship with his future medical mentor. However, once he started to attend some of his classes. Arthur Conan Doyle became captivated with the various academic lessons of this phenomenal medical marvel. During his college lectures, Joseph Bell emphasized the importance of close "observation" in making a diagnosis. To illustrate this, he would often pick a stranger off the street at random. And by observing such person for just a few seconds, Dr. Bell would be able to deduce the person's occupation and most recent recreational activities.

There were times when Dr. Joseph Bell would take notice of the type of dirt stains located on the bottom of a person's shoes, as well as the type of fabric that such person's clothing was made out of. In addition, he would obtain details such as the coloration of the person's face as well as any related smells that would emanate from the person's body. And in each instance, he would almost always be correct about deducing certain pieces of information about the person before such individual would even have the chance to explain their stories to him. In a way, Doyle was learning some valuable lessons about the "anatomy" of deductive observation.

In addition to working on living patients, Dr. Bell would also conduct various autopsies of random murder victims throughout the country. These deaths could not be explained or clarified by the local police departments themselves. During such times, Dr. Bell would look over certain parts of the person's body and try to take notice of specific things that most other people would not find significant. These small observations of the human body would eventually lead Dr. Joseph Bell to be able to deduce the manner in which the person had died and possibly where the person had died. In addition he might also be able to know general details about the possible assailants behind such crimes. These skills caused him to be considered a pioneer in forensic science, at a time when science was not yet widely used in criminal investigations.

Although Arthur Conan Doyle eventually graduated from medical school, he later attempted to start his own private practice out in the community in the hopes of taking care of his family. However, in the years to follow, he would never forget about the inspirational times that he spent in medical school, and how he was transfixed by his experiences with his renowned mentor, Dr. Joseph Bell. Although he himself could never truly reach the level of expertise and proficiency as his legendary advisor, Arthur Conan Doyle instead decided to use his experiences from medical school to serve as the basis for his future beloved character, Sherlock Holmes. Although Sherlock had only a basic level of understanding about the field medicine in of itself, he did possess a superb knowledge of biology and chemistry. He often would utilize the services of his trusted friend, Dr. John Watson, to assist him in many other related medical cases.

While I myself would love to be able to have the same astounding talents and abilities of the great Dr. Joseph Bell and the mythical capabilities of Sherlock Holmes, I am afraid that I will not be able to teach you how to diagnosis or deduce the personal information about a person simply by looking at them. Although this skill has been shown before on certain TV programs such as House MD and Monk, this type of gift cannot simply be taught from a book, and often requires years and years of painstaking efforts and dedication. However, before you give up on the idea of becoming a medical memory sleuth, here is one new challenge I have left for you to learn.

For this chapter, I will simply be teaching you how to **OBSERVE PHYSICAL AND BODILY SYMPTOMS** of a person, and not how to deduce their related medical conditions. I strongly urge those who read this book to **never engage in any behavior where you attempt to diagnose or refer people to various specialists based upon your**

own rudimentary assessment of their physical symptomology, without going through the advice of a licensed medical physician. Believe me; you don't want to tell somebody the wrong information about themselves that could invariably put their health or well-being at risk, simply by giving them the incorrect materials based upon your observations. As Sherlock would state, "When a doctor does go wrong, he is the first of criminals".

The next question that people tend to wonder is <u>what types of physical or bodily symptoms</u> we are going to be focusing on in this chapter. As many of you are probably not familiar with the countless number of medical terms that are usually studied by most medical school students, in this chapter we will only be focusing on the **12 MOST COMMON PHYSIOLOGICAL SYMPTOMS** that most people display outwardly on a daily basis. And the reason why we are choosing to use the *number 12* for this chapter is because the *number 12* has some historical relevance in terms of the field of medical science. There are usually 12 steps that are needed in order to complete <u>a full head to toe physical exam</u>, according to some nursing school programs. There are also 12 steps that need to be followed in order to prepare a patient to be prepped for a future surgery, according to some medical schools. There were 12 steps leading from the ground floor to the second floor of the infamous apartment building, 221B Baker Street, where our legendary detective sleuth used to live. And the words "Bell's Anatomy" are actually 12 letters long.

With regards to the **12 MOST COMMON PHYSIOLOGICAL SYMPTOMS** that often appear superficially on the skin of most human beings, the best way to memorize them is to use some of the same methods that were described previously in the chapter regarding word memory. In other words, rather than have you memorize what the actual physiological symptoms looked like, what you are going to do is memorize the words that can be used to describe the symptom that you are looking at. If you would like, you can take out any medically related workbook out there, and notice some of the pictures that are used to describe various bodily deformations. That way you can have a better understanding about how to actually visualize what you are looking at. I have included a list of the **12 MOST COMMON PHYSIOLOGICAL SYMPTOMS** as well as some images that I personally use to remember each ailment. You are free to make up whatever words or images you would prefer for any of the listed symptoms, as long as you are effectively able to memorize such words.

PHYSIOLOGICAL SYMPTOM	ASSOCIATED IMAGE
Burns	Burning flames
Suntans	Blazing sun
Bruises	Raw peach (bruise like a peach)
Cuts	Sharp knife
Scratches	Long fingernails
Flushness/paleness	Tomato/ghost
Swelling/lump	Large bubble
limps	Crutch or cane
Spots or marks	Clay handprints
Rashes	Red ashes
Scars or stitches	Crocheting a scarf
Bodily fluids (blood/discharge)	Fluid leaking out of a wall (color related)

The next step to take is to be able to learn <u>how to focus on observing the human body</u> in order to better notice any of the person's physiological symptoms. And for this, we will turn back to our previous lesson on <u>clothing</u> memory. This seems like a "fitting" situation, as not only does clothing cover a human body, but also covers the physiological symptoms as well. And in order to be able to do this correctly, you will have to be standing close enough to a person so as to be able to observe their clothing. So, in case you forgot about the lesson on clothing memory, let's revisit a lesson that might help you gain a whole new way of observing a person's physical health symptoms. And that method was **the FLASH method**. I have included the same example of the <u>FLASH method</u> below for your references.

*H*EAD	
*S*HOULDER	*S*HOULDER
*A*RM	*A*RM
LEG	LEG

FEET	*FEET*

Just as a reminder for those you may have not read through such chapter, the term <u>FLASH</u> actually stands for the <u>five areas of the human body</u> that people are most likely to be wearing clothing. The letter "F" stands for the person's feet. The letter "L" stands for the person's legs. The letter "A" stands for the person's arms. The letter "S" stands for the person's shoulders. And the letter "H" stands for the person's head area. Not only are these the five areas where people will most likely be wearing actual clothing, but these also are the <u>five areas of the human body</u> where most people will likely display any type of physical deformity or abnormality.

There are people out there who will also have bodily disfigurations in other areas that you might never be able to see. And while this might be something that a licensed physician would take notice of during a physical exam, you will most likely not be allowed to engage in such an intrusive inspection of the human body. So, for this method, you will only focus your attention on these five areas of the human body, as long as you are physically close enough to see the other person's skin behind the various layers of clothing that they are wearing.

If for example, I am observing a person in front of me, and I happen to notice that they have some *cuts* on their feet, I would remember that the first letter in the FLASH method is the letter "F". Therefore, I would put this information into the first room or location in one of my memory palaces. I would then create an image for the symptom "cuts" and would visualize this image in the first location of my memory palace. Then, I would move my eyes upwards and take notice of any symptoms that might be observed on their legs, if their style of clothing permits me to do so. So, if the person had a *rash* on their legs, I would create an image for the word "rash" and would place this image in the second location in one of my memory palaces, and so on.

Also, if you wanted to learn another method on how to remember which symptoms were located on which parts of the body, always remember the actual letters in the spelling of the word **FLASH**. By this, I mean that you could use some images that you have created for the <u>letters of the alphabet</u> and attach those images to the actual physical symptoms. So, if I wanted to remember the medical symptoms that I saw on a person's feet (cuts), I would remember the word "feet" starts with the letter "F". I would then attach an image for the letter "F" to the image of the medical symptom (cuts) that I noticed. Then I would place this information in the first location of one of my memory palaces, and so on.

Whether you believe it or not, no person is ever truly completely healthy. Even people, who take excellent care of themselves, will have some type of imperfection to present to others. Unless of course the person that you are looking at is wearing large and thick clothing, there will be at least one or two locations on their body where their flesh will be visible to the outside observer. However, before you really start looking for a person's physical imperfections, try to remember that *most people can be self-conscious or sensitive* about their bodies. They don't like other people's making fun of their bodily images. Make sure that you don't make any disparaging or negative remarks about the person, as this might offend them or make them feel angry. Instead, try to show kindness and compassion for the other person, and don't point out their demarcations unless they ask you to do so.

Another interesting point to consider is from a previous lesson that we covered earlier in the book called the **PAO method**, or person-action- object method of memory. In this case, sometimes if you notice some type of abnormality on a person's body, you can very much assume that such abnormality did not simply come out of nowhere. Most times, whenever we have some type of physical imperfections on our flesh, such as a scratch, bruise, or a bump, it is usually because of some type of interaction that we have had with an object or our own self doing. For example, if I see a person who has yellowish-brown burn marks on their fingertips, I usually will assume that this person has been smoking cigarettes recently. Or if I saw random scratch marks on a person's clean arm, I might only assume that they might have had some type of itch they were trying to scratch earlier.

In this case, try to realize that in order for a person to have had such type of physiological deformity occur on their bodies, it is most likely because such person had some type of interaction with some type of external object or internal ailment. Even flushness or bodily fluids can be influenced by outside forces of some type. Although you might never be able to truly ascertain what is responsible for a person's current presentation, you might try to take notice of any other related physical symptoms that a person is demonstrating, and try to "link" such information together in a certain way, such as PAO. This was the very same method that Dr. Joseph Bell and Sherlock Holmes always used to use when delineating a person's past activities.

For example, if I saw a person with cuts on their feet and a rash on their legs, I might have to assume that the person was not wearing the appropriate shoes in order to protect them from such injuries, and that there must have been some type of substance that was responsible for the rash on their legs. In this instance, I am describing a situation that occurred to me when I was much younger while I was on a camping trip. I noticed that one of the other boys that I was spending time with seemed to have cuts on his feet and a rash on his legs. While most of the other children could not figure out what had actually happened, I conjectured that this person had walked through the woods barefoot and had accidentally strolled through some poison ivy while coming back to camp. While there could have been many other different explanations for this particular scenario, it turns out that I just happened to be correct in this one instance. This is where I took my first "step" in the direction of learning about medical observation.

However, we are not going to be concerning ourselves with how to deduce where a bodily injury may have come from at this time. At this point, I would like to give you an opportunity to test your medical memory skills on some fictitious individuals who will be presented to you with certain types of medical ailments. I have included a list of **5 DIFFERENT PEOPLE**, each with **FIVE DIFFERENT PHYSIOLOGICAL SYMPTOMS** for each person. I have listed each person based on a number, as well as their associated symptoms listed below them. For this exercise, you will need two pieces of paper in order to complete this.

On the first piece of paper, you will need to write out all of the information that is presented to you below on the following chart. Try to make sure that you make the appropriate columns and rows as needed. Once you have written out all of the information, please flip this page over so that you cannot see it. Then, with the next piece of paper, create a table similar to the one that you just created, only leave this one blank. Make sure to label each column with a number and each row with a letter, so that you don't get confused between each person and each symptom.

Once you feel ready, flip over the first sheet of paper and memorize as much of the related information that you wrote down. You will have exactly **5 MINUTES** to memorize all of the information for all of the five listed people. Make sure that you have a watch or a timer with you. When you are finished, flip this piece of paper over again so that you cannot see the answers. Then, take a minute or two to review the information in your head as needed. When you feel confident enough with your recall, take out the second piece of paper and write down as much of the information as you can remember. Spelling does count, as well as leaving blank spaces; therefore each of these will count as an incorrect answer.

Since there are 25 pieces of information to remember, give yourself **4 POINTS** for each correct answer, for a grand total of 100 points. Be careful not to put the wrong information in for the wrong person, as this will also count as a mistake. Make sure to write down the time that it took for you to complete this assignment. Practice this exercise a few times a week to see how well you did on each repetition, and record your scores and times. Good luck and try to enjoy this unbelieve "a *bell*" experience.

	PERSON 1	PERSON 2	PERSON 3	PERSON 4	PERSON 5
F	Cuts	Bumps	Bodily fluids	Rash	Limp
L	Rash	Stitches	Bruises	Flushness	Burns
A	Marks	Limp	Burns	Swelling	Stitches
S	Suntan	Bruises	Lump	Suntan	Swelling
H	Bodily fluids	Flushness	Scars	Paleness	Marks

DAY EXERCISE	SCORE (PERCENT/ CORRECT)	TIME (MINUTES, SECOND)
FIRST DAY		
SECOND DAY		

THIRD DAY		
FOURTH DAY		
FIFTH DAY		
SIXTH DAY		
SEVENTH DAY		

AVERAGE SCORE=

AVERAGE TIME=

CHAPTER 12

"THE ADDRESS IS 221B BAKER STREET" (MAP MEMORY)

Previously I had referenced a very specific scene in one of the most recent BBC television shows depicting the life and times of our favorite literary detective. In such TV series, there is an initial scene where Sherlock Holmes first meets John Watson by chance at a local medical school laboratory. After observing Watson for just a few seconds and paying attention to his body language and physical stature, Sherlock is able to deduce various different aspects regarding the personal life of our beloved medical biographer, John Watson.

Once Sherlock has already finished analyzing the personality and medical status of his future partner in crime, he later infers that Watson is also looking for a potential roommate as he himself does not have an adequate place to live. Sherlock invites Watson to meet him later at his apartment the next day so that they can decide upon the terms of their future living arrangement. Watson is so astounded and amazed by Sherlock's deductive skills that he almost forgets to ask Sherlock what his name is and where he lives, as Watson does not know where to meet him. As Sherlock is leaving the room, he introduces himself as "the name is Sherlock Holmes and the address is 221B Baker Street".

Although we are not sure how familiar Watson was with the layout of the city of London, one could only imagine that with enough time and effort, Watson might be able to locate such address, and then begin the process of lodging with his new best friend. In the 1890's, there was no such thing as assistive technology that could help an individual to be able to locate a specific address anywhere in the world. However, in the 21st century, many of us have already become familiar with a certain type of assistive technology known as GPS, or <u>Global Positional System</u>. As the most common routine for transportation nowadays is simply getting into your car and then driving to a future destination, one of the greatest fears that most drivers face now of days is the unfortunate circumstance of getting lost. However, GPS is specifically designed to prevent such a dilemma from happening. This type of technology allows people to be able to navigate their cars throughout the various streets and roadways of all major cities, towns and villages throughout the world.

In addition, GPS also allows drivers to be able to choose more than one particular route to get from one location to another. And in the event that there is some type of roadway obstruction, such as a construction site or a detour, the driver can simply manually change course in any manner they chose. This machine will then "recalculate" a new route so that the driver is able to reach his or her final destination without getting sidetracked. In other words, it seems as though getting lost on one's "journey" is now a thing of the past for most people driving their cars on the roads these days.

Back when I was growing up, no one could ever have imagined such an amazing technological innovation such as this. To believe that a machine could help navigate a car to get across all types of terrains and obstacles in whichever manner the driver chose, was considered absurd by any and all standards. When I was a young boy, there were only three ways that my family would be able to effectively navigate our car towards its final endpoint. First, you could stop and ask for directions, which usually involved having to listen to another person dictate the directions to you. Second, you could ask someone else who was already familiar with the landscape about what was the best route that they preferred to use under such circumstances. And third, the most popular method that my family would use when planning out a future trip, was just to use a roadmap. That seems to be the "direction" that I taking in regards to this future chapter.

These days, the idea of using roadmaps to get from one location to the next seems almost as archaic as using a typewriter to write out a letter. We are so used to such advanced technology in this current decade, that we don't generally remember what it was like to have to rely upon simpler methods for such transportation related challenges. I still from time to time will utilize the services of a map in order to keep my instincts strong. I feel that it is not a good idea to overly rely upon the benefits of such advanced technology as there is always a chance that it might fail when you least expect it.

There were times when I was traveling around in my car and my GPS suddenly stopped working. This caused me great anxiety and fear as I was becoming too dependent upon its capabilities. However, I also always traveled with a roadmap book in the back of my car just in case such an event should occur. And if you are interested in ever purchasing a roadmap book of your own, they are still readily available at most major travel agencies as well as some larger gas stations across the country.

It is also important to always remain familiar with the dynamics and specifics of a roadmap just in case you find yourself experiencing a transportation related technological malfunction of your own. The problem is that many people now of days are not entirely familiar with the elements of a roadmap. Needless to say, a map is really just a piece of paper with various words, colors, symbols, lines, and numbers listed on it. If one is not familiar with what a map actually looks like, that person will not be able to effectively understand how to pinpoint one's current location as well as one's final stop accurately. However, do not be afraid as I am not going to be teaching you any advanced tactical related skills at this time. For this chapter, I will be teaching you the basic skills that you need in order to read a map, as well as some related skills that you can use in order to **MEMORIZE A MAP.**

Most maps, whether they are detailing the layout of a town, city, state or country, are normally made up of two distinct units of measurement. And those units of measurement are called **LATITUDE AND LONGITUDE**. **Latitude** is a geographic coordinate that specifies the north–south position of a point on the Earth's surface. **Longitude** is a geographic coordinate that specifies the east–west position of a point on the Earth's surface. One unit of measure dictates how high or low a particular locality is usually located on the map. Another unit of measurement determines how far to the left or right a particular site can be found on a map. By knowing the difference between latitude and longitude, as well as being able to connect the lines of both units of measurement at the same time, a person can more easily be able to determine where each labeled point on a map can be found. This allows the reader to pinpoint the exact location that they are looking for, rather than having to look over the entire map and hoping to get lucky.

Maps have been around for centuries throughout the whole world. Although many older maps were harder to read, and often had some geographic inconsistencies relating to certain locations, the idea of using latitude and longitude has been at the core for all map reading related challenges. Without knowing the latitude or longitude of a specific point, a person would never be able to remember exactly where they have been or where they were going. Regardless of any spelling errors or scratch marks found on any map, just knowing how to effectively use both latitude and longitude is usually good enough when it comes to plotting out a course along a typical route. It does not matter if you are familiar with the area, or if you are a tourist visiting for the first time, as long as you know how to make good use of latitude and longitude, you will never truly get "lost" in this world.

Sherlock Holmes was certainly a person who appreciated knowing as much as he could about the various streets and roadways of 19th century London. Even though there are now more roadways and entrances in London than there were back in the 1880's, Sherlock Holmes made it a point to become familiar with the city's variously famous travel points. Although Sherlock loved "lounging" around in the great city of London, he was also aware of some not so respectable neighborhoods and locations within London, or as he called them "that great cesspool into which all loungers exist". In one of the earlier episodes of the most recent BBC TV series, Sherlock and Watson make use of Sherlock's near photographic memory regarding the outlines of the streets of London in order to effectively capture a suspect.

During such episode, there is one scene where Sherlock and Watson notice that a suspected criminal is trying to get away from their current location. Such person is actively heading to another destination several blocks away by car. In just a few seconds, Sherlock is able to effectively recall the exact layout of the various streets in this particular neighborhood, and choses to chase after this fleeing suspect on foot, as he does not have a car at the time. Although he is clearly not as fast as the car that he is chasing after, Sherlock is able to remember certain short-cuts and passageways that inevitably help lead him to the next destination so that he can possibly capture this particular fugitive before such individual gets away first.

In another scene from one of the more recent movies depicting our renowned literary detective, Sherlock Holmes finds himself being released from a local detention center. He is then told that he has to go for a ride on a horse carriage to an unknown address across the city. In this instance, Sherlock is then blindfolded so that he cannot see where he is heading, nor does anybody tell him about the location of his future rendezvous. This is due to the highly sensitive nature of his future meeting. It is also revealed that his blindfold is not removed until he has reached his secret meeting place at last.

However, in this instance, despite the fact that he is securely blindfolded, Sherlock is already familiar with the current location of the detention center when he is then first released. And by using his other senses, such as hearing, feeling and even smelling, as well as his memory, Sherlock is able to determine which turns and movements the horse carriage was taking throughout the journey to the secret meeting place. Therefore, he is better able to deduce what streets the horse carriage was actually traveling on as it crossed throughout the city. This consequently makes it easier for him to calculate where exactly this "secret" meeting place is physically located once his blindfold is finally removed. His compatriots are amazed at his ability to blindly locate where he is currently sitting. They are also surprised by his highly developed observational skills by noticing the personal information of the people standing before him. And to think that such an act of navigational genius could ever have been accomplished without ever having to go to "school" in order to learn it.

Believe it or not, there actually is a real life "school of transportation" that is located in London, which first opened up around the same time as Sherlock Holmes. Such a school, which focused on the studying of the streets of London, is still in existence to this day. This particular facility for higher education is dedicated not towards the purpose of achieving a college degree or a learning certificate. It is actually a school designed to teach taxi drivers how to *successfully travel throughout each and every single roadway throughout the entire city of London*. Wow, that extent of information or "knowledge" regarding the layout of the entire city of London is an amazing feat in of itself.

Back in the 1880's, there were obviously less roads and passageways then there are now in London. However, this particular school was designed to help teach taxi drivers how to effectively maneuver throughout the entire city of London without ever relying upon any technological assistance. And this particular academic university is called "**The Knowledge**". These days, a London taxicab driver is required to be able to choose different routes in response to a passenger's request or various traffic conditions. The driver cannot stop to look at a map, rely upon a satellite, or even ask for directions. The "Knowledge of London" is an in-depth study course of a large number of pre-set London street routes. It also features all of the various places of interest that taxicab drivers in the city must be knowledgeable about in order to obtain a license to operate a cab.

A London taxicab driver must learn over 300 different routes throughout the entire city, as well as the locations of all major "points of interest". Such points of interest include places such as clubs, hospitals, hotels, theatres, government buildings, railway stations, police stations, courthouses, important places of worship, cemeteries, parks, sports centers, schools, restaurants and historic sites. During such trainings, these would-be cabbies, also known as *Knowledge boys* or *Knowledge girls*, usually follow these 300 routes throughout London while riding on a motor scooter, along with a clipboard fixed to their handlebars. Such clipboard shows them details of the streets to be learned for each particular day of class. Each related test of their memory of the streets of London is called an "appearance", as they are required to become familiar with that one particular route throughout London, for that one respective day. Classes are conducted several days a week, for several hours per day.

Each day, *Knowledge boys and girls*, without looking at a map, must be able to identify the two points of interest in London that their examiner chooses for them on that one particular day. Then they must be able to choose the shortest route to get from one location to the other. For each route, the applicants must be able to recite the names of the related roads to be used simply by memory, as well as any other locations where they have to make turns. They also have to remember what spots or intersections are located alongside each stage of their journey. It is the world's most demanding training course for taxicab drivers, and applicants will usually need to pass at least twelve different "appearances" in total, and get perfect scores on each and every one of them. The whole process itself takes **almost 3 years to finally graduate from the program**. These people definitely seem to understand how to navigate successfully around the complex "grid" that is the city of London.

Speaking of "grids", there is another lesson in the field of memory that can be applied to the science of memorizing maps. It is a system that has been used time and again by people who are responsible to have "knowledge" of various transportation systems, such as trains, subways, and mailing routes. You can usually see this particular "grid" in many major metropolitan locations, such as city police departments, railway stations, train terminals and emergency service arenas. And this particular mnemonic map, which was created back in the 1960's, is called the "**Memory Grid**". I have included a blank example of what a Memory Grid could look like.

	1	2	3	4	5	6	7
A							
B							
C							
D							
E							
S							
G							

As you can see, there are two different series of digits that are lined up in different ways. As you might remember from the previous discussion on how to read maps, the concepts of latitude and longitude can be used in order to find the exact coordinates of any specific location found on a map. When it comes to describing location information on a map, most people will start off with what the actual "latitude" is for a specific point. After this, the next piece of information is generally what the "longitude" is for that same location. Therefore, if someone wanted to know how to find a specific location on a map arranged as the Memory Grid, they would first locate what **row** (latitude A-G) is related to the destination, and then locate what **column** (longitude 1-7) is also related to the destination. There are also almost fifty different empty boxes located on such grid, all of which can be used to store vital geographic information in each one, such as the names of streets, buildings, locations or waterways.

Now for many of us, this particular system looks very confusing and overwhelming to say the least. Well, I suppose when looking at it in the way it was previously written, that might be the case. After all, this is not an actual list that can be memorized, but is it suitable for use in a Memory Palace. However, if you remember from our previous chapters regarding *numbers* memory and *letters* memory, I will show you another way to view the Memory Grid again, only in a more familiar pattern. Let's take another look at the Memory Grid, *shown in a different light*:

	A 01	A 02	A 03	A 04	A 05	A 06	A 07
	B 01	B 02	B 03	B 04	B 05	B 06	B 07
	C 01	C 02	C 03	C 04	C 05	C 06	C 07
	D 01	D 02	D 03	D 04	D 05	D 06	D 07
	E 01	E 02	E 03	E 04	E 05	E 06	E 07
	S 01	S 02	S 03	S 04	S 05	S 06	S 07
	G 01	G 02	G 03	G 04	G 05	G 06	G 07

Well, that seems to be a lot easier than the previous example. As you can see, in each box, the letter for the *latitude* comes first, and then the number for the *longitude* comes second. In this way, all you have to do is create an image in your head that combines both the letter as well as the attached numbers for each box. For example, in my previous chapter on letter memory, I gave you some examples of how I chose to memorize letters of the alphabet. So, for the letter A, I might choose to picture an "apple". For the letter B, I might choose to picture a "banana", and so on. And as many of you know from our chapter on numbers memory, when I see the number 01, I picture an image that is related to the letters **OA**, as this stands for 01. The image I have for the number 01 is a Boy Scout campfire. Therefore, if I wanted to remember the combination of A01, I would picture a large apple getting burned over a large campfire. And from that, I have an image for the box labeled A01.

Now, the next thing to consider is <u>what type of information</u> is actually located in each of the individual boxes. For this purpose of the exercise, I have kept each box empty of any related data. However, when you look at a map, you are bound to find lots of different pieces of information that are relevant to the geography of a specific location. Things like houses, buildings, rivers, and parks, are just a few of the various topographical items that can be found in the legend of any map used to this day.

However, if you are worried about how to actually remember the name of a particular street, that lesson was covered earlier in the previous chapter that discussed personal information. There were a few paragraphs that talked about how to memorize a person's address by using various imagery exercises. In case you would like to be reminded again, here is the chart that was used for such purposes. Feel free to use whatever images you would like in regards to remembering what types of streets are found on a map, as these are just my personal preferences:

TYPE OF ROADWAY	ASSOCIATED IMAGE
Alley	Alley cat
Avenue	Van with new sign in window
Boulevard	Large bull in a yard
Bi-Way	Ocean waves crashing
Causeway	Santa Clause on moving sleigh
Court	Legal court room
Drive	Automatic car stick shift
Highway	Toll booths

Interstate	Large battery
Lane	Yellow lines on road
Road	Concrete blocks
Route	Compass on GPS machines
Park	Swing set
Street	Stripes on a rainbow
Terrace	Terrorist cell
Way	Arms waving

With regards to memorizing the actual names of the streets themselves, there are so many different names for streets and roads out there in the world, that there is no real way to be able to come up with a rubric to help remember such information. In this instance, the best thing to do is to remember the lessons that were taught regarding the chapter on word memory. If you wanted to remember that a certain street or road was located in a specific box on the Memory Grid, you would try to come up with an image for the name of this particular street, and then attach it to the image for the letter and numbers associated with each box.

For example, if the major street that was found in box A01 was called Main Street, I would picture an image for the word "Main", and then attach this image to the word "street". And finally I would attach these images to the image I had created for A01. So, in order to illustrate how this works, when I think of the word "main" I think of a lion's mane of hair. Therefore, I would picture a large apple (A) getting burned over a fire (01), while next to this I would find a big lion's mane of hair (Main) colored with rainbow stripes (Street). And there you have it; I have created an image through the Link Method so as to remember that Main Street is found in box A01.

Now, one of the most difficult challenges in using map memory is being able to find a specific mnemonic method that can be used to store such information for future recall. As for me, I have found it much easier to use my Memory Palace for each letter of the alphabet, starting with A. For this, I chose to use at least the first several locations in my

Memory Palace to serve as the storage area for whatever information is linked to the letter A, as this is linked to latitude. So, for example, when I try to memorize what information is located for block A1, I already know that it reminds me of a big lion's mane of hair colored with rainbow stripes. I will then try to put this information in at least the first room in my Memory Palace. I do this because **A** is the first letter of the alphabet, and the number **01** is the first number in the numerical sequence. And then the next room in my Memory Palace would be reserved for the information located in box labeled A2, and so on. This is the "path" that I chose to use the most when it comes to such memory challenges.

However, there is more to a map than just a bunch of random streets and roads. There are certain "places of interest" that most people like to visit for various reasons. Places such as schools, hospitals, restaurants, and hotels are just some of the different places that you might find depicted on a map, depending upon what type of map you purchase. Sometimes you will find maps that barely let you see the names of the streets located in such areas; however the maps might overly delineate the locations of numerous "places of interest" for tourism related purposes. For this reason, I have included another list of the **20 MOST COMMON PLACES OF INTEREST** that can be found on a typical map, as well as the related images that I chose to use to remember such locations. If you can think of any other related places of interest that were not included on this list, please feel free to create more images for such reasons. Here is the list of the **20 MOST COMMON PLACES OF INTEREST** for your references:

POINT OF INTEREST	RELATED IMAGE
School/University	Graduation cap
Park/playground	Swing set
Cemetery/graveyard	Tombstone
Hospital/clinic	Stethoscope around a first aid kit
Police Department	Handcuffed person in holding cell
Court House	Judge bench with gavel

Jail/Prison	Ball and chain
Fire station	Fire ladder with hose
Restaurant/bar	Table with food and drinks
Hotel/Motel	Bellboy with luggage
Store/business	Cash register
Place of worship	Related religious symbol
Post office	Bag of mail
Gym/fitness center	Person running on treadmill
Body of water	Small boat on water
Airport	Airplane
Train/bus station	Station house with bench
Sports arena	Large trophy
Theater	Bucket of popcorn
Mall	Large parking lot

Well, at this point, I would like to quiz you on a fictional map of Sherlock Holmes's London. Be advised, this is a fictional map that is based upon many of the various names and terms that are associated with the stories of Sherlock Holmes. In real life, you would never find yourself looking at a map such as this at any major transportation related station. Normally, such maps are much harder to read, and have many more icons and symbols dictating various locations throughout. If you ever wanted to practice this particular memory technique yourself, you would have to mentally go over what the Memory Grid actually looks like in terms of letters and numbers. Some maps might be quite larger than the example of the Memory Grid that was previously mentioned. At its largest length and height, a Memory Grid could only be 10 rows long and 10 columns wide, according to the principles of letters and numbers memory that was shared with you earlier. Hopefully, you will not have to find yourself navigating through a map larger than this.

Okay, so here is the memory test for the fictional Sherlock Holmes's London map. I will be giving you another Memory Grid, but without the labels for the letters and numbers. You will need to make yourself familiar with the layout and structure of an actual Memory Grid. In each box, there is a fictional name or term that is connected with many of the stories of the Sherlock Holmes genre. For this exercise, you will need two pieces of paper. On the first piece of paper, you will need to draw out a blank Memory Grid with the same number of boxes that was included in the first example. In case you have forgotten what it looks like, here is the example of the Memory Grid from before:

	1	2	3	4	5	6	7
A							
B							
C							
D							
E							
S							
G							

Once you have copied down a blank version of the Memory Grid, **please fill in all** of the information that is contained within the fictional Sherlock Holmes' London Map. Be sure to include correct spelling and punctuation, as you will be graded on this assignment for such reasons. Once you are done copying down such information, please turn the first piece of paper over. Then, with your second piece of paper, create another blank version of the Memory Grid, as this will be your answer sheet. Make sure that you put in all of the related columns of numbers and rows of letters for this exercise. After you have created this second Memory Grid, flip this page over and prepare for your future memory challenge.

At this point, give yourself a few minutes to go over at least one or two of your memory palaces in order to complete this exercise. Then, once you feel that you are ready, flip over the first piece of paper with the Fictional Sherlock Holmes' London Map, and begin to memorize all of the information that you put down. You will be given a **total of 15 MINUTES** to memorize all of the data on this chart, so keep a watch or a timer nearby. Use as much time as you need for this assignment.

Once the timer goes off, or if you finish early, flip this sheet over again and give yourself **5 minutes to rehearse** the images in your head.

After your recall time is over, flip over the second page answer sheet with the blank version of the Memory Grid, and try to fill in as much information as possible. Make sure that you use correct spelling and that you put the correct names in the correct boxes. Since there are a total of **49 different boxes** on this grid, give yourself 2 POINTS for each correct answer. And if you finish before the allotted 15 minute time is up, give yourself another 2 points, for a grand total of 100 points. Feel free to practice this exercise a few times throughout the course of a week and see how well you improve your scores and accuracy. Good luck and have fun navigating yourself through this "*journey*" of memory.

Daniel Guilfoyle, LCSW-R

SHERLOCK HOLMES' FICTIONAL MEMORY MAP GRID

	1	2	3	4	5	6	7
A	Adler court	Baker Street	Dancing Man Post Office	Montague Road	Gregson gym	Napoleon art theater	Riding Thorpe restaurant
B	Paddington Train Station	Mycroft Airport	Goodge Street	Joseph Bell Hospital	Diogenes club	Gillette airport	Mrs. Hudson motel
C	Conan Doyle Clinic	Farnham Path Graveyard	Regents Street	Covent Garden Theater	London telegraph office	Moran Blvd	Bohemian church
D	Hyde Parkway	Moriatry Avenue	St. James Building	Thames River	Fleet street	Parliament bldg.	Lastrade bar
E	Jerome C. Store	Green Park	Pall Mall	Charing Cross Train Station	British army camp	Watson Medical school	Morton mall
S	Serpentine Field	Winchester Jail	Downing Street	North Humberland Avenue	Victorian clothes mall	Guardian sports arena	Sussex Downs farm
G	Dartmoor Horse Track	Victoria Train Station	Baskerville Dog Park	Scotland Yard Police Dept	Broad street	St. Bart's Hospital	Reichenbach falls

DAY EXERCISE	SCORE (PERCENT/ CORRECT)	TIME (MINUTES, SECOND)
FIRST DAY		
SECOND DAY		
THIRD DAY		
FOURTH DAY		
FIFTH DAY		
SIXTH DAY		
SEVENTH DAY		

AVERAGE SCORE=

AVERAGE TIME=

CHAPTER 13

EVERYTHING IS IN ITS PROPER PLACE (MNEMONIC NOTE TAKING SKILLS)

Although this is a book designed to teach people how to memorize and recall various topics of information more easily, it should be "noted" that, even under the best of circumstances, not all information is going to be printed out in a way that makes it easier for us to memorize in the first place. Whenever we are faced with the daunting task of memorizing data in the real world, it is either written out of order, or is often heard in such a manner that we tend to not know how to organize such materials. Unfortunately, unless of course you are preparing to enter a national memory tournament, where all the information is already listed out in front of you, this is just the way that it is for us.

A lot of times when we read something that is already written down on paper, it is not always easy to be able to piece together all of the information in a way where we can not only memorize it, but also to be able to know how each piece of data relates to each other. There is nothing more boring than to mindlessly memorize various pieces of material, one after the other, without having some idea about what we are memorizing or why it is important at all. And while some people are contempt with just being able to memorize information and recall it later on, it serves no purpose for us to be able to memorize things if we don't know how to organize such materials in a way so that we can later explain it to ourselves.

Sherlock Holmes did have had an extraordinary ability when it came to memorizing and recalling facts, as well as an unlimited amount of storage space in his enormous "brain attic" for such facts. However, when it came to physically storing such information in his office space, even by today's standards, he was quite disorganized. According to his roommate and partner in crime, John Watson, Sherlock can be remembered as a person who would keep his cigars in a coal bucket, as well as placing his tobacco in the toe end of a Persian slipper. He would also staple together his unanswered correspondences by stabbing them with a knife, into the very center of his wooden desk.

As time went on, his room became more and more disheveled to say the least. Thus, month after month his papers would accumulate, until every corner of the room was stacked with bundles of manuscript, all of which he forbade Watson from ever touching or removing for any reasons. These papers were not to be burned, or to be put away without Holmes' direct permission. Whenever his colleagues or friends would enter his office space and try to move around any of his related documents, he would often say *"everything is in its proper place"*.

When discussing the importance of how to organize materials inside of one's own head, or brain attic as he would put it, Holmes always felt that he considered a person's brain attic to be more like an empty attic that can only be stocked with a certain amount of furniture. He warned Watson as well as others that it would be foolish for a person to consider stocking up their "brain attic" with all sorts of useless or extraneous information, and to never truly sort out such information in any relatable fashion. He believed that it took lots of skill for a person to be careful about how much data or what types of data could be stored in such neural locations. In other words, a person would have to be selective about what types of information such person wanted to memorize in order to have a better understanding of the subject matter at hand.

Even Holmes was well known for his ability to organize and catalog the personal information that he felt was most relevant for many of the most famous people alive at that time. In several of his stories, whenever he was approached by certain members of the Scotland Yard Police in regards to investigating the crimes of specific criminals in London, Holmes seemed to have created a certain card catalog system (a reference to the

1980's version of library science), where he would collect and write down only the most important information about each person. He did this so that he could go back and read through this particular "file" and be able to recall most of the other important details about such person at a later time.

In one particular case, Holmes is informed about the kidnapping of the only son of a deceased high ranking political official. Once he is told the last name of this late civil servant, Holmes later opens up his cabinet drawer and retrieves a file on such person, as he has such records in alphabetical order. He later located a piece of paper that detailed most of the important and relevant information related to such person, such as their name, marital status, official title, as well as address and financial status. However, despite having such a well-organized file cabinet of such sorts, Holmes's main office can best be described as a large room full of endless piles of disorganized correspondences.

However, before you start to think that you are destined to live in such a disorderly world as the office space of Sherlock Holmes, I would like to reiterate an important point that was raised during my previous book, entitled "From Shrink to Think". In this book, I talked about the importance of *taking notes* on certain subjects of information in order to memorize them. And the reason why I chose to examine this subject is to give you an opportunity to have some ideas on how to simplify and organize certain topics of information so that you could easily memorize them for future references.

Note taking is a very valuable skill that can be used in the course of trying to memorize information that is randomly presented to you in a somewhat disorganized way. **Note-taking** is the practice of recording information from different sources and platforms onto a piece of paper. By taking notes, the writer records the essence of the information that they are reading, thereby freeing their minds from having to recall everything about such concepts. The person taking notes must be able to acquire and filter the incoming sources of data in a certain way, so as to be able to organize and restructure the existing knowledge they have about such information. The person is then expected to write down their individual explanations for the information in a manner that only makes sense to them. And finally, such person must be able to ultimately physically store and integrate the freshly processed material in some way for future references. This allows such person to be able to review their notes at a later date without have to reread through endless pages of information at their disposal.

Certain things such as names, dates, numbers, letters, and words, were often quite easy to memorize after practicing a few of the previous lessons. However, other materials such as book memory, speeches, historical events, and academic facts, are often not as easy to memorize due to the intensive nature of this data. Yet, I am going to teach you two different note taking methods that can easily save you a lot of time and energy when it comes to memorizing information that appears random in such nature. And those two mnemonic note taking techniques are called **THE FARLEY FILE, and the CHARTING METHOD**.

Previously, we touched upon each of these different concepts in certain chapters that dealt with specific memory techniques, such as personal information memory, as well as historical or current events memory. And it was shown how these different note taking techniques were designed to display the information in a different way so as to be able to better organize how to use your memory palace as well as how each piece of information was linked to each other. Still, it should be addressed that, even though these methods were discussed earlier, we did not get the chance to dive into how these techniques came about or how they actually work. Let's take a moment to discuss one of our most famous note-taking methods, **THE FARLEY FILE**.

A **Farley file,** created by legendary political consultant James Farley, is a set of records kept by certain individuals on specific people they have met before, spelled in a simple and specific fashion. Rather than reading through numerous pages about any one particular person, this systematic method was designed to summarize only the most important points of information to remember about a specific person. Whenever people were scheduled to meet with Franklin Roosevelt, James Farley would review their files and go over the information with Roosevelt. That allowed Roosevelt to be able to know such individual's spouse's name, their children's names, and anything else that had come out of earlier meetings with such person. The effect was powerful and intimate by both parties. And by remembering the names and personal data of all of the most important people that FDR was counting on to get re-elected on his campaign trail, James Farley was able to get FDR the political money and electoral votes that he needed to help him get re-elected more than once.

However, there are other related names that have been associated with the concept of a Farley File, or perhaps the title of the person who was responsible for memorizing such information in the first place. Back in the ancient times, it was not uncommon for a peasant, or a person of a lower class, to be given the responsibility of memorizing the names and titles of various people who were scheduled to meet with a ruler or a king perhaps. Such person was considerably called a nomenclator.

A **nomenclator** referred to a slave whose duty was to recall the names of the persons that his master had met during a related journey. Later his responsibility also consisted of memorizing the names of people in any other social context and included other socially important information such as the person's home country or socio-economic status in society. The term nomenclator also denotes a person, generally a public official, who announces the names of guests at a party or other social gathering or ceremony as they enter through the main doors during such ceremony.

However, it would surprise you to know that Farley Files can be used in other ways as opposed to just memorizing personal information or names and faces. For instance, several Farley files have been created for the purpose of memorizing information in biology. They usually include a list of the generic data, as well as the names of the species together with the origins or sources of these names. Sometimes they also include additional information, such as the literature distribution for such information. Here is one example of such a nomenclator.

• *Abronia* Gray 1838, Ann. Mag. Nat. Hist., 1 (5), 389. Rept, liz.

Abronia is actually the name of the species or genus of a lizard that was described by John Edward Gray in 1838. He wrote about such discovery in the journal entitled *Annals and Magazine of Natural History,* (Ann.Mag.Nag. Hist) as well as the numerical order of the Journal, and the page number associated with it. The entry ends with a note about the animal group that the genus belongs to, namely reptiles or

"Rept, liz". And as you can see, rather than writing out the information in a much longer and possibly confusing manner, this particular Farley File has condensed the information into a more abridged manner in order for the reader to be able to memorize it. To summarize this particular example, if someone were to try to delineate the information for themselves at a later date, it would look something like this:

(1) GENUS NAME
(2) NAME OF AUTHOR
(3) YEAR OF DISCOVERY
(4) NAME OF MAGAZINE
(5) NUMBERS ASSOCIATED WITH MAGAZINE
(6) TYPE OF GENUS

In this manner, rather than writing out all of the materials in the form of a very long sentence, the Farley File allows the viewer to summarize the basic information in a much more basic fashion. As long as the reader understands why the different articles of information are presented in the way that they are, it is usually very easy for such person to be able to rehearse and recall the data at a later date once they glance at the Farley File. And while there is no one specific way to create or organize a Farley File, the *actual manner* in which the person applies the Farley File should relate not only to the requirements of the individual subject, but also to the particular learning and comprehension styles of the learner themselves.

If you were going to try to memorize this information based upon the Farley File, all you have to do is try to remember the lessons that were discuss earlier regarding word memory, letters memory and numbers memory. In this instance, if you wanted to remember that the first piece of information that was listed is the name of the genus, all you have to do is come up with an image for the number 01 and place this in the first location in your memory palace. And then immediately next to this image, create another image for the term "genus", which sounds similar to the word "jeans". After this, you just think of another image for the word "Abronia", use whatever image you chose based upon how it looks and sounds. Repeat the same process for the next room in your memory palace for the category regarding the name of the author. And at this point, you will be able to fill out a few of your locations or rooms in your memory palace with information about this particular scientific discovery.

However, if you are interested in trying to remember this information without having to use your Memory Palace, you could also try to use the Link Method, though this might take longer to complete. In this instance, you would not have to worry about using numbers to remember different rooms in a Memory Palace. For example, if the most important point to remember is the *name* of the genus, let this be the first item in your linkage of images. In this case, you could then create an image for the term "Abronia", and then next to this image, create another image for the name of the author, and so on. As long as you are in agreement about the basic format and structure of your Farley File, you should have no problem being able to do this for many different scientific terms and words, as long as no two words are ever truly the same.

A second example of the Farley File can be connected to another method of organizing and learning that many people in the 19th and 20th century were very familiar with, when they visited their local libraries. It was a system of organization that could be found at pretty much every major library in the world, before the advent of computer technology and online databases. And this method was lovingly called the <u>Dewey Decimal System</u>. The Dewey Decimal System was a form of a card catalog system for libraries, where each individual entry in a library catalog contained bibliographic information, including the author's name, title, and location of the book itself. Dewey and others devised a system where books were organized by either individual subject, alphabetized based on author's name, or listed by the title of the book itself.

Each book was assigned a call number which identified the subject and location, with a decimal point dividing different sections of the call number. The call number on the card matched a number written on the spine of each book. There were three ways to organize each individual library catalog card: author, subject, or title. With regards to the author catalog, the card was listed alphabetically according to the names of authors, editors, or illustrators. For the subject catalog, the card was organized based upon the actual subject or field of study. And for the title catalog, the card was sorted alphabetically according to the article of the entries themselves. An example of such material can be found below this paragraph.

AUTHOR
TITLE
PUBLISHER
CALL NUMBER
SUBJECT

As you can see, although this style of cataloging is considered out of date by most 21st century standards, it can be easily used to memorize not only information regarding the subject of a book in a library, but also most other information that can be compressed into a simple yet similar structure. For example, if you wanted to remember the name of any one of the Sherlock Holmes stories in this fashion, all you would have to do is come up with images for the title, publisher and call number, if there is one. You already know the name of the author, and the subject could easily be considered crime fiction or some other theme related to the individual story. Some stories dealt with murder, others stories dealt with robbery or vandalism. Either way, you can easily come up with an image for any particular item.

So since you already know the name of the author Arthur Conan Doyle, and the first story that was ever written about Sherlock Holmes was entitled "A Study in Scarlet", all you would have to do is come up with some images that can be related to the words "study" and "scarlet". Once you have created images for the name of the author, as well as the terms "study" and "scarlet", you are ready to move onto attaching an image for the publisher. The publisher for such story was a small private publishing company called "Ward Lock and Company". Some of his other stories were published by a different company, but we will focus on this one for now.

For this one example, the next thing to do is to just come up with images for the words "Ward", "Lock" and "Company". You would attach these images to the right side of the images for the story name. Next, you would create images for the subject matter of the story. And in this story, there were instances of murder and robbery contained within the subplot. For this, you can easily come up with images for either of these terms. Therefore, you would attach images for the subjects of "murder" and "robbery" and place these to the right side of the image for the call number, if there is one. And there you have it, another great usage for the Farley File; the ability to remember information about any book or magazine article ever written, along with all of its most important relevant information.

Before you start to think that the Farley File is the only real method for note taking that is used in the field of memory, let me go back and reintroduce you to another topic that was covered both in this book as well as my former book. The next method of note taking that I want to get started talking about is a very famous and well used style called **THE CHARTING METHOD.** The **Charting Method** is a note-taking system that uses "charts" to condense and organize written notes. It involves splitting the paper into several different columns and rows, which are then filled with summaries of the information that is needed. This allows the person to have the information written in a way where they can more easily compare different topics and ideas between each other. A basic example of a typical note in the charting method is included below;

MAIN TOPIC	MAIN SUBTOPIC	NEXT SUBTOPIC	MAIN CATEGORY	NEXT CATEGORY

If you are interested in being able to use this particular method effectively in your memorization pursuits, it is easy to consider trying to memorize the information in the farthest left hand column in the first location in your memory palace. The reason for this is because, like all literature out there in the world, we tend to read sentences from left to right. And in this chart, the farthest left hand column represents the *first piece of information* that is to be memorized. That is why it is a good idea to start with the main topic in the first column of the Charting Method. This allows you to know where to start when determining what is the first important piece of information to memorize, as well as the upcoming related topics of information in the next few columns.

From the very outlook of this method, this appears to be very much generalized and oversimplified in nature. However, before you start to think that there is only one way to actually use the Charting Method, remember that each subject you use this on is different in of itself. Therefore, when you are preparing to put notes in a Charting Method format, instead of labeling your paper in the following way listed above, come up with answers to explain your choices for each column as far as what the actual subject means.

For example, if you wanted to be able to memorize information about one of the first Sherlock Holmes's stories such as "A Study in Scarlet", the *main topic* would be the actual name of the story. This information could easily be written in such a chart as long as you had enough room. In the next column, you could choose to state that the *main subtopic* of the story was the "introduction of the main characters, Sherlock and Watson", as this was their first story together. Then for the next column, you could state that the *next subtopic* was the related crimes that they were trying to solve, in this case both a murder and a robbery. Next, for the *main category*, you could chose to include where the actual story is taking place. Finally, for the *next category*, you might consider including the names or positions of the supporting characters for this particular story. An example of what this might look like is included below:

MAIN TOPIC	MAIN SUBTOPIC	NEXT SUBTOPIC	MAIN CATEGORY	NEXT CATEGORY
"A Study in Scarlet"	Intro of Holmes and Watson	Case of robbery and murder	Brixton Road	Gregson, "Rache", Ms. Drebber

By doing this, you have somehow managed to include only the most important information that is relevant to remember about what you have read. By reading through the story once or twice, just having this much information at your disposal should be enough to remind you of the variously different details and items that make up the composition of the story. Although this method is not designed for you to memorize all of the details about such story, just being able to remember these five major categories of information should be enough for you to suddenly recall all of the other related points of interest about such story as they come to your mind. For example, you could try to include images for the words "Study" and "Scarlet", and place these items in the first room of your Memory Palace. Always put the created images for the main topic in the first location in such palace. This will allow you to remember the first and most important item to recall, so that you can later attach other images into other locations to follow.

When it comes to putting words into the actual charts for the Charting Method, there really is no need to write out complete sentences or phrases. This method was designed to work for you with just the bare necessities of information, as the chart will allow you to have the structure needed to remember the rest of the information. It is actually much easier to remember the data based upon the rows, as opposed to the columns. This is due to the fact that many of us are used to reading words in a sentence, going from left to right.

Well, in this case, you would start to memorize the first item at the top left of the chart, and then proceed to memorize the next item located to its right, and so on. That way, you are memorizing information topic by topic, not category by category. If you want to, you could also add another column to the far right side of the chart, in order to allow you to be able to create notes if you wanted to. This would make it easier to write notes that are relevant to the topic at the end of such chart.

The Charting Method is only good for taking notes on subjects that have factual information, as well as subtopics that are directly compared to each other, and information that can be compartmentalized into tables. Therefore, the one major downfall of this particular note taking method is that it does not help the reader who is interested in something other than *memorizing actual printed facts*. This will not benefit the reader who is interested in memorizing information that is subjective or philosophical in nature. As you might remember earlier from the chapter on personal information memory, I gave an example of what the Charting Method of Note Taking would look like if it were applied to actual history or current events information. Here is the example again listed below:

WHO	WHAT	WHERE	WHEN	WHY	HOW

However, the best point about the Charting Method is that it is the best and easiest method to use when a person is interested in studying the written or printed "facts" about almost any available subject out there. Subjects such as art, music, politics, business, sciences, social sciences, law, mathematics, literature, as well as computers, can all be studied as long as the person who is interested in learning about such field, is willing to study the major events that are related to the history of such field. As long as the field of study that you are interested in contains famous people's names, major events, worldly locations, historical dates, major themes, as well as procedural changes, this method will ultimately give you the frame work needed to put such information down on a chart and therefore be able to memorize in a much quicker and easier format.

Let's say for example that you wanted to know more information about the author of the Sherlock Holmes series, Sir Arthur Conan Doyle. If you wanted to memorize facts or other particulars about him personally, you might consider memorizing his name, what he did that was so famous, where he lived when he did it, when he completed such task, why he chose to do so, and how he managed to complete such task. For this, we already know the name of the author himself. And we already know that he wrote the series of Sherlock Holmes stories.

However, it should be noted that he wrote the first book entitled "A Study in Scarlet" in the town of Southsea- Hampshire, located in England. Also, he wrote such story in the year of 1887, when he was only 27 years old. The reason why he chose to write such stories was because he was struggling in his current private medical practice, and wanted to see if he could make some monies out of such productions. And finally, to better explain how he came up with the idea for his stories, he had based some of the characters in this story upon other people that he had met from his earlier life, such as his former college medical professor.

So, if you wanted to condense such information into the earlier example of the Charting Method, it might look something like this:

WHO	WHAT	WHERE	WHEN	WHY	HOW
Arthur Conan Doyle	Wrote "A Study in Scarlet"	Southsea Hampshire England	1887	Medical practice struggling	Based characters on medical professor

In this example, if you wanted to remember the name of the individual that you thought was famous, you could create images for his or her name and place such images in the first location of your Memory Palace. Then in the next location or room, you could place images for what famous activity such person actually did. This would include making sure that you pay attention to the associated verbs or action that is related to the individual in question. Next, you would try to create images for the name of the place where such historical event occurred, and place these images in the third room or location in the Memory Palace.

After this, you can place images for the associated historical dates in the next room or location of your palace. In the next room or location in your Memory Palace, you would try to create images for the reasons why this person engaged in their actions at the time. Try to come up with some tangible or reasonable explanation for their actions so that you can better conceptualize such information in your head. And finally, in the last room or location in your Memory Palace, create images for the actual methods used by such person to commit the action that they had committed.

At this point, you already have a good idea about how and why to use either the Farley File method or the Charting Method of Note Taking. The two most important points to consider before going ahead and using such mnemonic note taking techniques, is first to decide which of the two methods is best suited for your current learning endeavor, and secondly to create a rubric or a format that you will use for either method. Like I said earlier, the best thing about using either of these methods is that there is no one specific layout or design that you have to utilize for just one purpose.

You have to decide the manner in which you organize and structure your information so that it best suits your own personal learning needs. Don't worry about what other people are using for their own personal endeavors; just decide how you prefer to learn information and what is the easiest arrangement that allows you to learn such information. This is a decision that will have to come from you and not from someone else. Sit down and give yourself some time to really think about your own personal learning inclinations, and try to set up either of these note taking methods accordingly. And remember what Sherlock Holmes once said, "Never stop learning, because life never stops teaching".

CHAPTER 14

"YOU SEE BUT YOU DO NOT OBSERVE" (OBSERVATIONAL SKILLS)

In one of his earlier stories, Sherlock Holmes is first seen sitting down in his office along with his faithful companion, Dr. John Watson. They are both going over some of the various theories that Holmes prefers to use when he is trying to understand the intricate details of various crime scenes. During one of their initial discussions, Watson asks Sherlock to explain how he is able to take notice of so many different peripheral items whenever he enters any given residence. Sherlock simply looks at Watson and explains that he chooses _to pay attention to the specifics_ that most other people tend to ignore. In order to further illustrate his point, he asks Watson whether or not he knows the exact number of "_steps_" there are in the staircase leading up from the main floor all the way towards their respective 2nd floor office space.

Watson is initially perplexed by this query, as he does not know the answer to it. Sherlock is bothered by the fact that even though Watson has walked over the same staircase each and every day, that he still does not know the exact answer to the question. When Watson is not able to give Sherlock an adequate response to this coveted inquiry about the staircase, Sherlock simply replies that there are in fact 13 different stairs that lead from one floor to another. When Watson apologizes to Sherlock for not knowing the answer to the question, and explains that he can't understand how he could have missed such an obvious detail, Holmes looks at Watson and states "you see but you do not **observe**". Also, it seems as though the number 13 plays an important part in this lesson, as you might figure out when spelling out the word OBSERVATIONAL.

For many people who work in the fields of physical security, law enforcement, military intelligence, and penal corrections, there is a model that these particular individuals have been very well trained in, an idea that most other people in the world are completely ignorant of. And that concept is **OBSERVATIONAL AWARENESS**. By this I mean, being able to walk into a room or other physical location, and being able to pay attention to the most important details that surround you, regardless of your familiarity with your environment. Many of us don't generally know what to look for when we are outside or in unfamiliar territory until it's already too late. However, there are certain individuals out there who are taught and trained to spot trouble before trouble spots them.

To display observational awareness means that a given individual should be able to see, understand and comprehend their natural surrounding environment, regardless of where they are. Whether you standing in a room, building, office, facility, or any other natural habitat, the ability to know your surroundings as well as where to spot danger, is a vital skill to have in order to better survive in an unsafe world. Police officers, security guards, special operators, and *"covert spies"*, have been trained to see the things that most of us don't pay attention to, or simply the things that we "do not observe". The earlier example of the interaction between Sherlock and Watson regarding the number of stairs between the different floors in their household is another example of such skill. Sometimes we just don't take notice of certain things around us as we feel that such materials are not important to pay attention to. This leads us to either forget or sometimes overlook a certain detail that someone else might have already noticed before us.

One of my favorite examples of a person using observational awareness comes from another one of my other favorite movie characters, Jason Bourne. This is a film series that chronicles the action packed adventures of a lone amnesiac character known as Jason Bourne, who is not only an assassin and a spy, but also a former special operations soldier. He is an individual with many enhanced abilities that seem almost superhuman to most people who watch these movies. Whether it be his ability to fight off multiple adversaries in hand to hand combat, being able to drive any type of vehicle under hazardous conditions, or his ability to blend in and disappear whenever he goes out into public, this particular individual just seems to be almost unstoppable no matter what he does or where he goes.

There is a very important scene in one of the earlier movies, where our main character is sitting down in a diner along with his new girlfriend. He is explaining to her that he is already keenly aware of his current surrounding environment, without getting distracted or having to use too much effort. He states that even though he has never been to this particular restaurant before, and has only been sitting down for a few minutes, that he is already aware of where all the exits are located, how many people are in the room with them, as well as already having had the time to memorize all of the license plates numbers of all of the cars in the parking lot. And strangely enough, he is able to do all of this in just a few short minutes without getting overwhelmed by his surroundings. And yet, despite this extraordinary display of observational awareness, he still can't even remember what his real name is.

Such a scene vividly describes the inherent nature of observational awareness. It is not about what you see, but rather what you "observe". The two terms seem similar, but in reality they are not the same. When you look at something, you are simply focusing your attention and gaze upon such object. When you observe something, you are actually taking notice of this object and perceiving something specific or unique about it. Unfortunately, this is not an instinctive ability that can occur all the time all on its own. We have to mentally make ourselves <u>want to pay attention</u> to something more in order to be able to observe it. Yet it takes next to no effort to actually physically stare at something. In order to see something, all you have to do is turn your head and aim your eyes directly towards your intended destination. However, in order to actually *observe* something, you also have to make yourself curious or inquisitive about the object that you are actively viewing.

Sherlock Holmes was well renowned for his ability to notice the details that most other police officers merely did not pay attention to during his investigation. Details such as what type of ash stains were on a person's hat, the different lengths of scratch marks on an individual's shoes, or the detailed coloring of the dirt along a specific bike trail, were just some of the clues that never escaped the eyes of our ever watchful legendary detective. Whenever everyone else seems to be looking in the wrong direction, Holmes always knew where to look and what to be aware of. In other words, he simply knew what he already wanted to look for and ultimately where to find it.

There is a universal concept that makes the most sense when it comes to memorizing information. Most people who read this book will have to realize that if you are considering undertaking the challenge of memorizing information, regardless of the situation, there is no way that you will be able to do so if you don't try to prepare yourself for the task at hand. No matter how gifted or unique your mnemonic abilities may seem to you, if you don't *prepare* for your future memory challenges for at least a few minutes, you will never be able to get started on the right path. And as a Boy Scout, I always believe in "being prepared"

I myself have tried to improvise at times during my various memory challenges, only to find myself making mistakes and missing valuable details. This made me realize that while you might not exactly know when you are going to be challenged to memorize certain pieces of information, it is often a good idea to get yourself mentally prepared to memorize information just in case the challenge finds you unexpectedly. In other words, before you attempt to memorize something, you need to know ahead of time what you want to be looking for in order to be able to memorize it in the first place.

When I was working in prison, I was taught several valuable lessons that enabled me on how to spot certain details amongst the inmates throughout the prison. There were certain things I was shown such as what part of a cell provided the best place to conceal contraband, what types of clothing inmates were likely to wear in the event of a future fight, or even what position an inmate could take when standing in line for food in order to avoid conflict. These were just some of the things that I never truly paid attention to when I first arrived at the prison. Nor did I believe that these factors could be considered important points when making decisions that would ultimately determine my safety. As one officer once said to me, it was important for me to *pay attention* to the details that did not seem to fit within the particular situation, as these were often the first signals that danger was looming. He often stated, "If it doesn't seem right, keep it in your sight".

I could easily understand the connections between these random independent variables, as well as how they were related to overall security measures. However, when I would question the officers about why these particular details were important in the first place, they would explain to me that knowing about these specific items somehow allowed them to have the advantage of being able to prevent altercations before they even occurred. Knowing what to look out for was the only thing that they could do to maintain some level of security in such a wildly unpredictable place. Once they explained this type of situation information to me, I had a better understanding of how they were able to do their jobs on a daily basis. This was the way that they were trained to do security in their own respective environments, particularly in prison.

However, there are several other different types of observational awareness modules in the world that employ many different steps to master them. Various concepts such as the <u>OODA LOOP, BEING LEFT OF BANG, CONDITION YELLOW, AND CHECKING YOUR SIX</u>, are just some of the different ways that certain people are trained to think when they have to make difficult decisions in sometimes dangerous situations. However, this book will not be addressing with you how to attain certain skills that are needed in order to come home alive when faced with deadly obstacles. For this book, I have come up with a brand new technique that will allow you to have a much more enhanced ability to be able to *memorize information* in just about any situation you find yourself in. Whether you are completing memory tests from the confines of your home, or memorizing information out in the real world, there is one specific mnemonic that I tend to follow in order to better "prepare" myself for any future cognitive endeavors. And that technique is referred to as the **H.O.L.M.E.S TECHNIQUE**.

I know that most of you are probably not entirely surprised that I have chosen to use the last name of our literary hero in order to better conceptualize this process. While this is not an official observational awareness training technique, it is a simple memory mnemonic that I tend to use in order to better prepare myself for having to memorize information. And it involves at least **6 DIFFERENT STEPS** that a person would need to take in order to have a better chance of being prepared to memorize information. The six different steps of the **HOLMES TECHNIQUE** are as follows:

> **H**= here and now mentality
> **O**= observe your surroundings
> **L**= listen to the sounds
> **M**= memory technique to choose from
> **E**= envision the information
> **S**= say it out loud to yourself later

The first letter of the **HOLMES** method is "**H**", which stands for being in the "here and now mentality". By this I mean that in order to be able to better memorize information more effectively at home or in the community, it is important to be focused on what is happening around you right now at the present moment. Be aware of where you are and what you are doing, and not focusing on anything else. Try to ignore your own inner voice if it is telling you to think about things from your recent past or soon to be future, as this will be distracting.

I have found that if I want to have any chance of being able to successfully memorize materials that are set in front of me, I cannot allow myself to be distracted by what is going on within my head. If there are certain noises or sights in my own mind that are diverting my attention from the task at hand, I will make every effort to ignore them to the best of my abilities. I will only be focusing on what is required of me at the present moment. In addition, I may also engage in some deep breathing or meditative relaxation so as to quiet my nerves and alert my inner senses.

The second letter of the **HOLMES** method is "**O**", which stands for "observe your surroundings". For this step, after you have calmed your mind and grounded yourself by being in the present moment, the next thing to do is to pay attention to not only what you see but also to what you "observe". Focus on things as if it was the first time you had ever truly noticed them. Don't just look at an object or a piece of data as if you had already seen it before. Make yourself interested in what you are looking at so that you have the right motivation to pay more attention to such facts, rather than just simply seeing such object with your own eyes.

Try to ask yourself questions about what you are looking at so that you can make yourself want to pay more attention to the information in front of you. This makes you better able to memorize materials as you are actively making yourself pay more attention to the data around you. You are also giving your full concentration on what it is that you are actually memorizing at the present moment. Try to quiz yourself on certain themes or patterns in the information that is presented to you, in order to better conceptualize what you are really seeing.

The third letter of the **HOLMES** method is "**L**", which stands for "listen to the sounds". In this respect, I urge you to pay attention to whatever sounds or noises you can hear within your current environment. This will most likely apply if you are trying to memorize information outside your house, as most people who chose to engage in memorization activities at home will often try to limit any distracting sounds at the time. If you are in the outside world, and you have already taken notice of the visual cues that are in your field of vision, try to squint or close your eyes for just a few seconds.

As long as you have taken the time to pay attention to the most important visual details around you, closing your eyes for a short time will not be a problem. Try to decipher whether the resonances around you are high pitched or low pitched, as well as whether the sounds are loud or quiet in tone. Attempt to do this for at least a few seconds, in order to get a baseline as far as what the standard decibel level feels like in such an environment. This will allow you to have more information to memorize at a later time.

The fourth letter in the **HOLMES** method is the letter "**M**", which stands for the "memory technique to choose from". For this step, after you have already taken notice of the important visual and auditory information that is around you at the present moment, it is a good idea to decide which particular memory technique you wish to use in order to memorize such data for this specific situation. Remember, there were several different methods that were described throughout the book. You can try to use any one of them, depending upon your comfort level with each of them, as well as how much and what type of information you are preparing to memorize.

It is not easy to anticipate which methods you are going to use ahead of time. However, if you have some idea about what to expect when you are faced with a certain memory task, just give yourself a few seconds to decide which technique you feel most comfortable in using at such moment. Also, make sure to go over any related memory codes and Memory Palaces when you have a chance, as this will more than likely be applicable to the task at hand.

The fifth letter of the **HOLMES** method is the letter "E", which stands for the need to "envision the information". For this sequence, it is best to try to create images or graphics in your head depicting each and every piece of data that you are trying to memorize. Try to use your inner instincts and think of the easiest and most outrageous images that you can conjure in your mind, as long as they are graphic and vivid. Make sure that your images POP in your mind, and that you chose to use whatever point of view, or POV, you feel most comfortable with.

By this, I mean that you need to decide if you want to memorize the information by creating images that are going from left to right, as well as what locations you feel are most convenient to be used for such purposes. Sometimes, there will be locations within your Memory Palaces that might not be easy to use when it comes to placing various images in certain orders and sequences. Once you have both seen and heard all of the information that you need to memorize, and have chosen a proper mnemonic technique for such purposes, make sure you know how to envision such information in your head so that you are better able to organize it and recall it later on.

The final letter of the **HOLMES** method is the letter "S" which stands for being able to "say it out loud to yourself later". By this I mean that after you have already memorized the information that is directly in front of you, you should find a quiet place to go somewhere, and give yourself a minute or two to mentally go over the information again for the purposes of rehearsal. Review and rehearse the materials that you have collected quietly to yourself, or ask someone else to quiz you on certain pieces of information that you find most relevant.

If you need to, try to sub-vocalize the images in your head, by giving the characters in your Memory Palaces some dialogue between themselves, so that your images are both visual and auditory in nature. Try to mentally go over the "lines" that are being uttered between any of the related images or characters in your mind. Go over such information in your Memory Palace both forwards and backwards, until you feel confident that you have successfully memorized all of the material to the best of your abilities. This will be the last step that you have to take when using this preparatory method. As Sherlock would say, "nothing clears up a case so much as stating it to another person".

And there you have it, the **HOLMES Method** being broken down into the various "steps" that are necessary for the purposes of effective memorization. In summary, when you first find yourself preparing to engage in such type of memory challenge, regardless of where you are, try to silence your mind and allow your brain the chance to relax. Don't feel the need to impulsively worry about seeing and hearing everything around you, let your mind ease itself to the point where the information will come to you. Then, allow your eyes to focus on all of the stimuli around you that actively gets your attention. You will notice that your eyes will lead you unconsciously, without your brain or body dictating the direction and flow of your peripheral vision. Next, after you have taken notice of all that you think is necessary at the moment, decrease your field of vision and allow your ears to pick up on the auditory clues around you for just a few seconds, so that you are actively aware of any related information cues for such effect.

Then make a choice as to what memory technique or method you are most confident and comfortable in using once all of the information has been imputed through your eyes and ears. Sometimes, the decision as to what method to choose from will take some time and effort on your part. Other times, the particular technique will come automatically to your mind without any conscious efforts. Either way, chose which method you feel most comfortable in using for such purposes. Finally, after you have used the specific mnemonic technique that you feel is most appropriate for the task at hand, go back and mentally review the information by quietly saying it aloud to yourself or by having someone else quiz you about such data. This allows you to challenge your brain in order to analyze the information in various ways. And from there, you have <u>successfully used the HOLMES method</u> in order to be better "prepared" for the task of memorization. These "steps" almost seem quite straightforward, or as Sherlock would say, "Elementary".

CHAPTER 15

SELF-CARE TECHNIQUES, HOLMESIAN STYLE

Although I am not a crime solving superhero like Sherlock Holmes, I do believe that in order for a person to be able to take on the challenges of their everyday life, it is important for such person to take care of their own body and mind. We are all creatures of this earth, and we need to make sure that we supply ourselves with the basic necessities of life in order to be more productive members of society. Certain things such as physical and mental maladies can impede our ability to take care of ourselves and others around us in our daily lives. However, it must be mentioned that, unless of course you are fortunate enough to have other people provide you with various homeopathic services at home, the main person responsible for taking care of your body and mind is ultimately <u>you</u>.

I have always believed in the concept of the body and the mind having some type of universal relationship with each other. No matter how complicated and complex the body and mind seem to be, there is an inherent causality between what happens in one realm as compared to what happens in the other. As a therapist and a person who has to take regular care of his own health, I truly adhere to the philosophy that "the body fuels the mind, as the mind fuels the body". In other words, if you truly want to be capable of doing the things that Sherlock does on a daily basis, it does not matter how many times you successfully memorize information. The most important step to take before you even consider taking on the challenge of any memory related task, is to first *take care of your own body and mind*, so that you are healthy enough to accomplish the job at hand.

The brain is still a very complicated and problematic area of study for most professionals in this world. It seems as though we as a society have an exceptional amount of information and knowledge about each and every major vital organ in the human body. Things such as the stomach, kidneys, heart, lungs, nervous system, spinal cord, and reproductive areas, are just some areas that have been studied for generations and generations. And although we are currently in the 21st century, we seem to know a lot more about each of these major anatomical components than most other people did back in the days of Sherlock. Even Dr. Joseph Bell would stipulate that there were certain aspects of human anatomy that he was not inherently familiar with. And despite the extraordinary advancement of medical technology and awareness in the past thirty years, there is still one organ of the body that we are still perplexed by to this day; the human brain.

When a person does not take care of themselves both physically and mentally, the brain has an unusual way of retaliating in a variety of ways. Certain medical and psychiatric symptoms such as hallucinations, delusions, racing thoughts, manic episodes, changes in dopamine and adrenaline, as well as cognitive impairments and chronic deficiencies, are just some of the ways that the mind reacts to the body when it is not properly taken care of. Despite the billions and billions of neurological cells that make up the chemistry of the human brain, it is no "mystery" to conclude that the brain is a very delicate and tantalizing part of the human body.

Yet, even when we make one poor decision about what type of activity we engage in, or what type of substance goes into our body; our brain has a *cryptic* way of reacting towards us. And when this happens, it makes the idea of trying to engage in any cognitive related activity seem almost impossible. Thankfully, many of us do make some attempts in our daily lives to take better care of our body and mind so that we can be productive throughout our regular lives. Yet, despite his encyclopedic knowledge of various subjects throughout his life, Sherlock Holmes did not seem to truly believe in the critical necessity of mind-body self-care. In this respect, what we are doing to do is, instead of focusing on more ways to become like Sherlock Holmes, we are going to try to learn from his past mistakes about self-care.

Sherlock Holmes may have been a genius in his own mind, but the one thing that he always seemed to be lacking knowledge of, was the ability to take care of himself in an appropriate and healthy manner. It always seemed as though, whenever a major case found its way into his humble little apartment on Baker Street, Sherlock would usually pay too much attention to the particular details of such crime, and would neglect the basic care of his own body. Whether it was him staying up to the late hours of the night, starving himself by not eating his meals for days at a time, to sometimes even experimenting with addictive narcotics, Sherlock always seemed to have an array of different ways to avoid the concept of self-care. There were three main ways that Sherlock tended to neglect the care of his own body and mind: **engaging in social isolation, not eating and sleeping properly, and experimenting with brain boosting narcotics**.

Throughout his many *journeys* solving crimes, along with his faithful companion Watson by his side, Sherlock would usually devote all of his time and energy to the case at hand. And despite the physical toll that such adventures took on his body, he was more concerned with solving the case than we was concerned about taking care of himself. John Watson, a medically trained physician, would often mention to Sherlock that he needed to take better care of himself in various ways which Watson felt were vital to his overall general health. There were times when Sherlock would isolate himself in his apartment when there were no major cases to work on, and would normally avoid going outside into the fresh air of the streets of London.

During such times of hibernation, Holmes would try to find various ways to occupy his mind by engaging in random scientific and psychological challenges that he thought would be useful in gaining knowledge that he could one day store in his precious "brain attic". Whether it was examining the flying patterns of insects around his room, to experimenting with various narcotics on their family dog, Sherlock never considered how important it was for him to live a healthier and more fruitful life outside the limited boundaries of his criminal related pursuits.

Although this might seem like quite an unhealthy pattern of behavior for most people, Sherlock seemed to be aware of a very important concept when it came to being able to keep his mind sharp and focused. Despite the fact that he sometimes chose to avoid social gatherings and other related recreational activities, he did seem to be able to challenge his brain to solve various problems and theories that he had conjured up just to see if he could rise to the challenge. He truly hated the idea of being left alone in a room with nothing to work on and no activities to stimulate his brain. One time he explained to Watson that his mind "rebelled against stagnation" and that he often craved "puzzles and work". This is one particular self-help technique that Sherlock was absolutely correct about. And that concept is the idea of <u>brain boosting activities</u>.

Certain things such as completing a crossword puzzle, balancing your budget, reading a book, drawing a picture, working on a Sudoku problem, or just putting down your phone and turning off the TV, are just some of the ways that people chose to challenge their minds rather than just sitting on the couch and becoming tired due to lack of activity. It is always a good idea to try to engage in some type of cognitive brain challenge at least once a day, as long as you are feeling healthy enough to do so. Such continuous stimulation allows your brain to grow and nourish itself, as you are challenging your mind to solve problems or complete tasks that you would not otherwise be able to do if you were inactive. Doing this on a regular basis can help you to not only remain mentally awake, but can also help to decrease the chances of succumbing to various neurological deficits, such as dementia and Alzheimer's.

Another area of his life that Sherlock seemed to avoid taking responsibility for was the need to <u>eat healthy and get a good night's sleep</u>. There were times when he would starve himself almost to the point where he could not walk or run a certain distance. He stated that he would do this in order to make his brain work harder and avoid getting tired and sleepy by eating a heavy meal. He realized that his brain could operate to a certain level if he chose not to eat a specific amount of food for such day. What he did not realize was that, despite his temporary abilities to solve various crimes at the time, what he was really doing was impacting his health in a slow and progressive way where he would later need even more stimulation just to keep up with his usual pace.

In addition, Sherlock was known as a night oil due to the fact that he would like to stay up late and either listen to his violin, or read through the various papers scattered around his room. This would often annoy his roommate and partner in crime, John Watson, as Watson would frequently ask Holmes not to keep him up at night as he needed to get some sleep for the following day. Although Sherlock was well aware that all human beings need to get some rest in order to survive on this planet, he would often push the boundaries for how much sleep he needed if it meant having the opportunity to gain the upper hand in any particular case.

For this reason, I am advocating that in order to better take care of yourself, you should try to avoid doing the things that Sherlock would do in such similar situations. For that I mean, if you truly want to be able to memorize information more clearly and effectively, you will need to eat healthy food and get an appropriate amount of sleep. All of us are aware of what happens to our minds when we either eat too little or too much. If we chose not to eat enough food during the day, our minds may initially be slightly stronger for a short period of time. However, once that minor burst of energy goes away, ultimately we begin to feel weak and tired, as our bodies are starting to break down and lose energy.

And when this happens, the brain eventually falls in line with the decline that the body is experiencing. On the other side of such notion, when we eat too much food before any major event, the blood supply in our bodies is directed towards our stomach and away from our brains for a short while. This causes us to be become sluggish and tired for a while, as even though we are now well nourished, our brains do not have the adequate amount of blood needed in order to properly focus on the task at hand.

For this sake, I state that if you are planning to engage in any memory related challenge in the future, it is a good idea to make sure that you chose a time that does not interfere with your daily meal schedule. I prefer to do my memory challenges either just before I eat a large meal, or at least 1-2 hours after I have finished consuming my food. The reason why this tends to work is because your stomach has already had enough time to digest the food that it already has processed, and your body is then more suitable to engage in a more cognitively challenging manner.

There may be instances where you are out in public and you want to try to test yourself to a mnemonic undertaking. For this instance, it is a good idea to make sure that you are properly hydrated and healthy by drinking the appropriate amount of liquids needed in order to help nourish your body and provide you with enough fluids so that your stomach does not get sluggish at times. Although you can never be sure when you might have to put your mnemonic skills to the test out in the real world, it is always a good idea to carry around some type of beverage with you so that you can remain hydrated and relaxed when needed.

By the same token, it is also a good idea to make sure that you get an adequate amount of sleep in order to make sure that you are able to handle the challenges of the next day. There is no real exact amount of time that a person needs to sleep in order to consider themselves mentally healthy. For most adults, it is recommended to get at least 7-8 hours of continuous sleep a night, although this amount might vary depending on many different personal characteristic of the individual in question.

Although it is not for certain that a specific amount of sleep will guarantee that a person is able to memorize information better or more accurately, it is certainly guaranteed that if you do not get enough sleep at night, your brain will be too tired to be able to concentrate and focus as you would normally expect it to. Whether we realize it or not, even when we think that we are strong and capable of handling whatever challenges come our way, when we don't sleep enough the night before, we discover that our brains do not have the same level of motivation and attentiveness as we would expect it to have under normal circumstances.

Another area of concern that needs to be addressed based upon the lessons of Sherlock Holmes, was his reliance upon <u>variously different substance and narcotics</u> that he would use in order to help fuel his mind and enhance his senses. Certain affluences such as opium, cocaine, nicotine, and self-made elixirs, were just some of the experimental devices that Sherlock used to see how well he could perform under pressure during the course of some of his investigations. Again, his trusted friend and colleague, Watson, who was a well-trained medical physician, would often lament Holmes regarding his own fears concerning the addictive consequences of continuing to use such substances.

However, despite his friend's worries regarding his addictive behavior, Sherlock believed that if he could heighten his cognitive skills only temporarily, just for the purposes of solving a very important case, than whatever side effects he might feel during the course of any future withdrawal would be worth the discomfort. Often times, Watson, would have to lecture Holmes about his over-reliance upon such substances as opposed to using healthier and safer alternatives, such as regular medications and various homeopathic ingredients. Still, despite his warnings and admonitions, Sherlock remained somewhat addicted to these various nootropics, often to the point of near danger.

In this case, what I am advocating for you to consider is to be careful about the possibility of engaging in any type of behavior where you might want to consider using various nootropic or other cognitive enhancing materials. Although there are numerously different kinds of nootropics out there on the market and in most local drug stores, it is generally a good idea to consult your local physician about the pros and cons of using such alternatives, as some people are more sensitive to certain chemicals than others. I for one am very used to using one certain generic nootropic substance that many of us are already familiar with, and that is caffeine.

This is the most basic brain boosting liquid on the planet, as it gives you some sense of energy and euphoria for a certain period of time. However, try to be careful about how much caffeine you ingest during the day, as you should also consult with a physician about what is a healthy amount for you based upon your personal medical history. Some people are also very vulnerable to this particular beverage, and should try to avoid drinking too much during the course of the day, as this can lead to various medical ailments and side effects.

Despite Sherlock's apparent lack of concern for his own individual health and well-being, he did engage in two different practices that allowed him to strengthen the core of his brain without putting the rest of his body at risk. These two particular homeopathic habits were his everlasting love of playing violin music, and his proverbial love of

Daniel Guilfoyle, LCSW-R

smoking his tobacco pipe in his favorite armchair. However, while these might seem like innocuous alternatives compared to some of the other methods that Sherlock utilized in his daily endeavors, what he was really doing was using two different yet remarkable self-care techniques that are specifically designed to help calm and sooth the brain during times of stress.

First of all, I have discovered that, while there are many different types of music out there for one to listen to in this ever-changing world of melodious harmonies, it turns out that there is one specific type of music that when listened to, will somehow both enhance and enrich the human mind through its specific tones and qualities. And that type of music is measured by its <u>binaural beats</u>. For most people out there, this is a whole new concept to understand, as many of us are simply content with just finding a basic relaxation CD out and simply listening to it. While this may sound like a modest and efficient way to calm the mind, it should be noted that precise levels of binaural beats have been proven to affect the mind and body in very specific ways.

The binaural beats that a person perceives are the frequency difference between the sound waves entering the left and right ear. All the music that we tend to listen to in our daily lives is quantified by using a certain unit of auditory measurement known as a *hertz*. The binaural tones of relaxation music should be at frequencies lower than 1,000 hertz in order for the human brain to detect the binaural beat in the first place. Binaural beats that are at a frequency of 13–30 hertz may help promote concentration and alertness. Binaural beats that are at a frequency of 7–13 hertz may encourage relaxation and stress reduction.

There were many times when Sherlock would pick up his favorite violin, and begin practicing whatever chords or melodies he wished to practice, time after time again. However, when Sherlock was playing the violin so close to his head, he often would relax and focus on the particular moves and methods that he would perform with his hands in order to create certain musical tones and melodies. Even though most people assumed he was intentionally focusing on the actual notes that he was playing, what Sherlock was really doing was taking more interest in the actual tones of each note he produced. Though he would

204

sometimes make mistakes or not perform to the level of a maestro, he certainly allowed himself to become transfixed by the various tenors and sound qualities that he emanated from this one simple instrument. And by focusing on the sharpness and flatness of the music that is presented to us all, we too can become more transfixed by the melodic sounds that we hear as opposed to concentrating on the lyrics or dialogue that is present in most music.

Another interesting technique that Holmes utilized when he was feeling overwhelmed by the numerous facts and information that were presented to him, was his ability to sit alone in his favorite armchair and light up his infamous pipe with certain types of tobacco leaves. While I am not advocating that smoking is the best method to use when it comes to relaxing the mind during times of stress, I should point out the fact that, while Holmes was not aware of it, he was actively engaging in another method of relaxation that many of us are already familiar with. And that method is called meditation.

Although many of us always seem to conjure up an image of a person sitting in a particular position with their eyes closed, and making many inaudible sounds or chanting noises, this is far from the truth when it comes to active meditation. You do not need to practice any particular type of religious faith or achieve any level of spiritual transcendence in order to be able to meditate correctly. All you need to do is find a quiet place to sit and rest, close your eyes, and allow your mind to focus its attention to your breathing and your bodily position. You don't need to smoke a pipe like Holmes did, however he would do this in order to pass the time while he was quietly sitting in his chair, ruminating about whatever particular evidence was baffling him at the time.

Sometimes he would be sitting in that chair for hours, during which time he would be engaging in what he referred to once as "a three pipe problem". By this he meant the amount of time it would take for him to actively smoke three whole pipes of tobacco in one sitting. So for that reason, sometimes it is a good idea to find a place in your home or office where nobody can bother you, and just allow yourself to get comfortable for a certain period of time so that you can give your mind a chance to work freely without any constraints or deadlines to concern itself about. This allows your mind the chance to not only work at its own pace, but also to sometimes recover information that was once thought to be lost, but was ultimately just buried beneath the surface in the brain.

While this is not a concise list of self-care or homeopathic approaches, it is nevertheless a simplistic guide on certain ways that you can learn to take better care of yourself both physically and mentally so that you are better able to use your brain for any related mnemonic challenge. Simple things like eating and sleeping well, engaging your brain in certain boosting activities, using safe and healthy nootropic materials, listening to certain types of relaxation music, and trying to find time to sit and quietly meditate about the events of the day, are just some of the ways that you can take better care of your mind not just for the purposes of having a better memory, but also for your own overall physical health. If you don't take good care of your physical and mental health, your brain will be useless to you in your future aide-mémoire undertakings. In the end, this will affect your ability to succeed in your future brain related workings. And as Sherlock would say, "I cannot live without brain-work, what else is there to live for?"

CHAPTER 16

CONCLUSION

Well, this certainly has been quite an adventure to say the least. Who would have thought that there would be a book out there that focused specifically on the inner workings of the mind of the great Sherlock Holmes? There have been many books written about him in certain stances, such as how to think like him, how to observe like him, and even how to act like him. However, there has yet to be a book that focuses entirely on how to **MEMORIZE** like him. Although I cannot take credit for any of the other Sherlock Holmes's related materials that were mentioned earlier, it has been proven through various stories that a lot of the methods and mnemonics that were explained earlier in this book were actually employed by Sherlock during his random crime solving adventures.

Despite the fact that Sherlock was almost mythical in his abilities to deduce, decipher, analyze, observe, and scrutinize whatever information was put in front of him, this was not an ability that he was genetically born with. Although there are some people out there in the world who have natural abilities such as photographic memory, as well as those who are human calculators, speed readers, forensic profilers, and gifted analysts, there any many other people who struggle to keep up with such extraordinary individuals. And believe it or not, Sherlock Holmes did not actively get into the field of deduction and crime solving until he was already a college student. It seems as though had he not actively advanced himself throughout the field of early forensic science, Sherlock Holmes might never have become the source of such world renowned fame and notoriety which has continued to entertain audiences for decades.

For many of us, the superhuman abilities of these select few people seem almost mythical due to the belief we have that we might never truly be able to do what they are doing. I have to admit that when I first started out in the field of memory enhancement, I had my doubts that I would ever be able to make any significant improvements in my own memory which would allow me to get a glimpse into the world of these cognitive superheroes. However, I certainly hope that, by reading this book and by practicing the exercises and activities that were listed in each chapter, maybe one day you too will be able to demonstrate some similar talents or traits such as those demonstrated by the brilliant consulting detective.

It is important to remember that the techniques that were described in this book are not just for the purposes of solving crimes, as it would be expected if one truly wanted to be more like Sherlock Holmes. Things such as the Memory Palace, the Link Method, the Substitution, as well as the Farley File and the Charting Method, can be applied to virtually any particular subject or theme out there in the world. As stated earlier, you can choose to use these methods for educational, vocational, and even personal reasons.

These types of techniques have been used by students in higher education in order to get better grades on tests and quizzes. People who are working professionally in their respective businesses, have found that they can use some of these skills in order to get work done faster, be more productive while meeting deadlines, and sometimes get raises in pay or possible promotions. And then there are those who wish to use such skills in their own personal lives in order to get along better with relatives, such as making more friends, being more aware of the personal lives of loved ones, or being able to take care of oneself out in the community.

The most important idea to think about is to decide what area of memory you would like to improve upon the most. You are free to choose as many as you would like, as several different subjects were presented to you. Perhaps you want to improve your memory of numbers, names, personal information, or even dates and facts. The choice is yours depending upon what area of your life you would like to improve the most. If you feel up to the challenge, see if you can try to improve your memory in all related areas, but don't expect to be able to master everything all at once, as this might take a while. It may take months or even years to be able to be proficient in all related subjects that were listed in the book. Some might come easier than others, but don't be discouraged throughout your "journey" into the field of memory. Continue to work hard on any areas that you are struggling with and go over the intricate lessons that were described for each chapter, so that you are refresh your memory at times.

Another area to consider questioning is to decide whether or not you want to be more like Sherlock Holmes himself. I am not espousing that you should take it upon yourself to go out and establish your own consulting detective agency. Nor am I suggesting that you try to solve major crimes throughout the country, unless of course that is your intention. What I am trying to say is, the more you practice and train in each of these various areas of memory improvement, the more you will start to realize that you are getting a little bit closer to realizing the genius of Sherlock Holmes. He did not always seem to care about the praise and accolades that he received from his colleagues and peers; however most of us are probably different than that. Once we start to get better at improving our memory and sharpening our focus, most people around us are inevitably going to notice, and will probably be quite impressed and astounded.

Throughout your "journey" into the field of memory improvement, you will start to notice certain strengths and weaknesses in your performance. I just want you to realize that although these methods have been around for centuries, it does not guarantee that each person will be able to memorize information as easily and quickly as the other. There may be some subjects that you struggle with, and you will start to notice that there might be certain mistakes that you make in the process. Rather than getting frustrated or giving up on the idea of mnemonics entirely, it is a good idea to pay attention to your areas of weakness and try to make a mental note on what you are doing wrong. Otherwise, you might start to find yourself getting irritated and resentful at times.

Once you start to learn where you need to improve, focus more of your attention and energy towards those areas and try to figure out how to avoid making similar mistakes in the future. Whether it is how fast you memorize information, the exact order or sequence, as well as the point of view that you use in your envisioning processes, there is always room for improvement. Remember, even Sherlock Holmes made a few mistakes in his past cases. He would often ask Watson to remind him if he was going to make the same mistake twice, as he would often use such a case as a benchmark for future progress.

Just imagine how amazing it will feel when you are able to demonstrate such amazing mental abilities to others in the public. Most people cannot possibly imagine another person being able to perform such incredible memory related feats in the real world, unless such person is a genius or a child prodigy. The point is that you don't need to be either of these things in order to learn these techniques; otherwise it would have been a waste of your time to read this book at all. I will never forget the looks on my loved ones faces when they first started to see me perform random memory related acts. Most people are both inspired and amazed by those who can show us the limitless capabilities of the human brain. For it makes us want to know how they are able to do it, and if possible, if we ourselves can one day do the same. This is especially good if you are surrounded by people who think that they are smarter than you, for they will not expect you to be able to have such remarkable talents such as these.

Well, that is all I have left to teach you about the field of memory improvement and mastery. As some of these lessons might be new and original, others can also be found in my previous book "From Shrink to Think: A Mental Journey Through the Memory Journey". I too am a huge Sherlock Holmes fan, and have been so for several years. I have read most of his books, have seen multiple movies and TV programs, and have even collected certain amulets and charms that are related to the renowned British detective. And since I am aware that Sherlock possessed an incredible memory as well as other related cognitive skills, I felt it best to share not only some of my own personal wisdom, but also some of his own "private intelligence", in order to help you to realize your potential in being able to think more like Sherlock Holmes.

I wish you luck in your future memory related endeavors. I hope that you have enjoyed this journey as much as I have, for I know that Sherlock would have felt the same. I am indeed "Sher-locked" by the incredible lessons of memory that I have written about in this book, and I hope that you will feel the same too. Until then, I hope to hear back from you soon as you navigate throughout your own memory adventures. Or as Sherlock would say "if convenient come at once, if inconvenient come all the same". Take care and DON'T FORGET.

INDEX OF TOPICS

Printed in the United States
by Baker & Taylor Publisher Services